Happy

EXMOOR AND THE QUANTOCKS

The coast near the Valley of Rocks, Lynton

EXMOOR AND THE QUANTOCKS

A Walker's Guide

by

JOHN EARLE

CICERONE PRESS
MILNTHORPE, CUMBRIA

ISBN 1 85284 083 8

Cicerone books by the same author:
    Walking on Dartmoor

Front Cover:
    On the Exmoor coastal path below Sugarloaf
    Photo: Walt Unsworth

CONTENTS

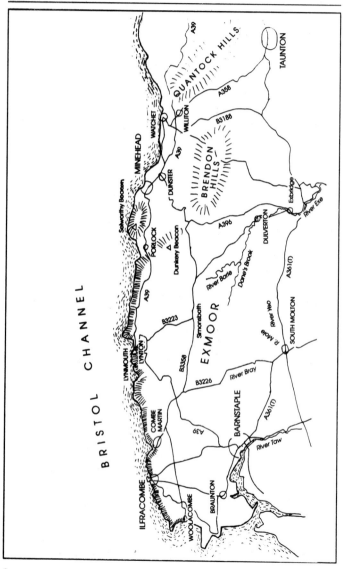

INTRODUCTION

I SUPPOSE that it is not a very convincing way to start a book on Exmoor by stating that I am really a Dartmoor man! But those of you who have read my book "Walking on Dartmoor" will know that I have a very deep affection and knowledge of Dartmoor having lived near or on the moors for nearly 50 years.

Of course it is a senseless exercise to compare the two, for their characters are completely different for a variety of reasons. Firstly and most importantly Dartmoor is a wild, rugged, granite moor with the stark tors peeping through, while Exmoor, though composed of many rocks, is mainly sandstones and other sedimentaries of the Devonian period. It is these underlying rocks that give Exmoor a softer, more gentle and intimate landscape with deep, secret valleys often densely wooded.

I have become really excited and fascinated by what I have seen and found out about Exmoor during the research for this book and I hope to share with you some of that enchantment.

However, there are a few things that have caused me unhappiness and though I shall be returning to some of these gripes later on, I thought that I had better get a few of them out of the way fairly quickly as they have some bearing on the rest of the book!

For example, I deplore the way in which a lot of the open, high land of Exmoor has been encroached on over the years and how many of the moorland areas have been walled or fenced in. This means that for a lot of the time I could not get away from the feeling that I was walking in an enormous field with fences or walls all round me! But before all the farmers start complaining, let me make it clear that I appreciate that for economic farming these days, the reclaiming of moorland as "newtakes" is vital, but all the same I am sad to see it and to find that it has been allowed to happen, over the years.

The result of all these fences and walls is that there has to be gates through them to give access, a very laudable thing. But in order to make sure that people use the gates, as indeed they should, then there are endless signposts and way-marked paths even in the really wild and lonely places. I suppose that it is to do with getting a right balance, but I did not enjoy finding signs, however tastefully they are made, telling me where to go and how far it is, almost everywhere I went. It takes away the feeling of adventure and exploration.

This, then, is perhaps one of the major differences with Dartmoor (and here I go again comparing them) for I found Exmoor a much more gentle, safer walking area - and why not, for those who perhaps do not want the fierce challenge that the heart of Dartmoor gives on both calm and stormy days? And again I had better ward off the anger of Exmoor lovers who will be quick to tell me that storms on The Chains, for example, can be just as ferocious as Dartmoor, but all I can say is that the paths, the walls and the signposts will soon help you back to safety, which you would never find on Dartmoor.

The Quantocks, even though they are a lot smaller than Exmoor, seem to be very much more of a defined, detached, high moorland area with great charm. But, as with Exmoor, they have enormous problems with four-wheel drive vehicles churning all over the tops, following, or not following, the many tracks that lace the open moorland.

But enough of the negative side. What impression did Exmoor, the Brendons and the Quantocks have on me? How best to introduce you to the area and to sum it up in a way that will make you want to explore it with me?

I think that the greatest delights are the contrasts, the huge variety of countryside and beauty that you will find on Exmoor, all crowded into the small area of 265 square miles.

. Many people who come to Exmoor may well rush to climb Dunkery Beacon, as the Everest, the highest summit of the moor at some 519 metres (1,704 feet). The access is easy with many tracks running like spokes of a wheel from the huge cairn on the highest point. This could well be an excellent introduction to Exmoor, for from the summit you can see some of the finest views. Much of the moor stretches away below you. But come here very early in the morning or at sunset for at other times it is a popular place and often crowded.

Look away north from Dunkery and you will see Wales across the Bristol Channel even as far as Gower and the Cambrian Mountains, the Brecon Beacons and the Black Mountains. The River Severn leads your eye on towards Gloucestershire and the Cotswolds. Farther east on the far side of the flat, fen country of Somerset, you might be lucky to see the low line of the Mendips, while on the Somerset/Devon border the Blackdown Hills are visible. Turn south-west and there is Dartmoor with its jagged tors and on really clear days you could imagine that you can see Bodmin Moor in Cornwall before you let your eye wander back to nearby Exmoor itself.

Around here the moorland is all heather and skylarks but tucked away in the folds are the sheer, steep, wooded valleys and indeed from Dunkery the hill drops precipitously down to Horner Water where in summer the forest lies like some heavy, green mist filling the bottom of the combes.

Beyond, you will see the flat, low flood plain of the Vale of Porlock with its pattern of fertile fields and further behind still Bossington Hill and North Hill rising steeply above Selworthy church.

So Exmoor then is full of fragmented contrasts both of sight and sound. Of course like so many moorland areas there is the song of the thrilling, trilling skylark bubbling with its cascade of sound and hopping with feigned wounded wing to lead you away from its nest. You will also hear the plaintive curlews, while lapwings fall about the sky, swooping within a few feet of your head, uttering their strangled cry if you get too close to their nests. You might hear blackcock if you are lucky and, if you are even luckier still, you might hear and see stags belling in the autumnal mists.

Water is everywhere in the squelching peat hags of the Chains or Exe-head, and from them the trickles tinkling down to the sparkling, rushing streams and rivers of the wooded valleys. The Exe, the Barle, the Lyn, Yeo, Mole, Bray, Avill. The musical names go on for ever like their flow, gentle and serene at most times but surging and violent in storm, sweeping and slaughtering as they thunder and roar down north to the Bristol Channel or south eventually to reach the English Channel.

Man was here in early times and you will find the mystical stones, graves and barrows of prehistory, like the stepping stones of Tarr Steps. You will hear about the Knight family and will already know about the Doones! There are old, deserted iron mines full of ghosts now and there is modern farming and the hardy Exmoor farmers.

There is nothing more exciting than to put up a herd of red deer and watch them flow up the steep coombes, turning to look at you and see what you are about, before the old stag gathers his ladies and moves them on. And what about stag hunting, for some feel that it is a vital and essential part of Exmoor life?

You won't need much luck to find the distinctive, true-bred Exmoor ponies with flowing mane and sooty muzzle; they are often seen on the high moor grazing quietly or galloping away on the sky-line frightened by some real or imaginary danger.

There is the delight of discovering that Exmoor National Park runs right up to the north coast where it ends in the shimmering Bristol Channel and towering cliffs well over 1,000 feet high as well as weird corners to explore like the Valley of Rocks.

Of course tourists flood here in their thousands in cars and coaches looking for the Doone Country, souvenirs, "kiss-me-quick" hats, cream teas, ice creams, postcards and the rest. But thank goodness there are little pockets of Exmoor where the more discerning can still find complete loneliness and solitude, with the breath-taking beauty.

I should like to share with you, through this guide, some of the magic and mystery of Exmoor and take you in these pages to some of the places that have fascinated and entranced me. And for those of you who have neither the desire or the inclination to walk, I hope that you will be able to come with me, in your imagination, and see what I have found out about Exmoor, through this book.

The Geology and Formation of Exmoor

IN THE INTRODUCTION I mentioned that the underlying rocks of a region determined the character of a landscape and countryside and that Exmoor was made up almost entirely of sedimentary rocks. This word means, as you might expect, that they are rocks that were formed from deposits laid down at the bottom of oceans, lakes or rivers; sediments, in other words.

It could be said that Exmoor was a tableland intersected by a great many deep valleys that have been gouged out by streams and rivers which, except in the north and west, all flow into the River Exe. This erosion and weathering of a landscape is a continuing process and the speed at which it happens depends on the age and the hardness of the rocks. On the whole sedimentary rocks are softer than igneous rocks like the granite that made Dartmoor.

So the underlying rocks of Exmoor were laid down in the geological time known as the Devonian Period which occurred between 415 and 350 million years ago and the Carboniferous Period, 350 to 280 million years ago. These deposits were formed on the bed of some ancient ocean and resulted in the slates, grits and sandstones we find today. Enormous pressures and movements took place in the Earth's crust at this time causing titanic tilting and folding into the synclines and anticlines that rose up to become the rocks of Exmoor. Rocks that have changed their character by heat or pressure are called metamorphic rocks and some of the mud underwent enormous pressure to become the slate that stretches out to the Brendons and which was quarried for many years. The rocks of the Devonian Period also contain iron and this was mined in several areas on Exmoor and the Brendons.

Exmoor is almost wedge-shaped, like a piece of cheese with the sheer, humped-back cliffs of the north plunging over 1,000 feet to the sea, while inland the countryside drops gently south down towards the rolling Culm Measures of central Devon.

The upland soils of Exmoor are poor and unproductive, mainly peat on which only heather thrives, while below the peat a layer of impermeable clay and iron pan makes for wet and waterlogged walking. On areas such as The Chains the peat is of considerable depth but in most others it is shallow, brown and spongy in the wetter areas, while in the drier regions, where the water can drain away, it is black and decomposed.

The valley soils are a type of brown loam, again with an orange, silty clay underneath but in spite of this they drain well and when dressed with lime become quite fertile. Towards the north-east of the Brendons there is an area of Red Marls and New Red Sandstone where after millions of years of erosion the valleys lead down to a fertile alluvial plain.

In Britain the three Ice Ages have always to be considered and while the ice-cap and glaciers never formed as far south as Exmoor, much of the area was covered with deep snow and ice in winter. During the summer thaw a lot of the topsoil containing mud, rocks and stones slid over the surface forming, in some areas, what now looks like man-made terraces.

In the way that the rocks give rise to the character of a landscape so the rocks and soils determine the vegetation (the flora) that grows and can survive in a region; this I suppose also gives the character to the landscape. And of course the vegetation will dictate which animals (the fauna) can live in any particular area.

Vegetation

THE VEGETATION of the area we now know as Exmoor in very early times, from 12000 B.C. onwards, can be discovered by the most interesting study of pollen found deep in the peat and also carbon dating.

Slowly the climate of Britain began to warm up as the last Ice Age retreated and with it the tundra. So by between 7500 and 5000 B.C. seeds carried by the wind or birds from much farther south took hold in the area and there is evidence of the dwarf willows and birches, which I have seen within the Arctic Circle in Baffin Island, growing on Exmoor in these early times. As the climate again warmed, pines, hazel, alder and oak all took hold. The moist, warm centuries encouraged other broad-leafed trees such as limes and elms to flourish with the oaks, even as high as 1,300 feet and stumps of bog-oak have been found in the peat at this height.

By about 200 B.C. we would recognise the climate as being like that which we have today with occasional south-westerly gales, heavy rain but warm summers and sun. It is this final change of climate that made it impossible for trees to grow on the high open moor because of the strong winds, but they survived still in the valleys from those early times. So it is our present climate coupled with the soils that is now responsible for the existing vegetation of Exmoor and also the fact that man felled any trees that did survive on the high moor making regeneration impossible even if the climate had allowed it.

Man, as you might expect, has tampered with nature, felling many trees, ploughing up land, draining other areas, so that the natural vegetation changes. But in his favour, he has also planted trees although, in modern times, this has not always been well received, as sometimes serried ranks of conifers march across the skyline and fill what were once lovely valleys with dark gloomy rows of trees for commercial use.

Not only the cutting of trees, but also forest husbandry and planting had all started centuries before the Forestry Commission's attack on our moors and mountains! The Saxons in the times before the Norman invasion lived on or near an Exmoor that had no trees on the uplands, for the climatic reasons given earlier, but they used the densely wooded valleys of oak and beech as a source of material for their buildings and as food for their herds of pigs. They understood the value of wood and forests and had learnt, in other words, woodland management that included coppicing.

In the early nineteenth century the threat of an invasion by Napoleon hung over Britain with only the wooden walls of our navy to stop him. Oaks were needed for these wooden ships and attempts were made and thwarted to fell some of the huge oaks on the estates of a certain Sir John Trevelyan at Nettlecombe Park in the Brendons. The outcome of all this was that the Surveyor General of Land Revenue offered the quite extraordinary opinion that large areas of Exmoor could be planted with oak, ash and beech, another idiotic example of a government department making suggestions, probably from some warm office in London, that were completely impracticable. At this time, in 1818, the Knight family come into the picture and I shall be coming back to them and how they planted many of the beech hedges which are now long lines of trees that are so typical of many parts of Exmoor.

In a survey commissioned in 1965 Geoffrey Sinclair, the chief field officer of the Land Use Survey of Great Britain, divided Exmoor into the five vegetational regions:

1. *The Coastal Heaths* with hills climbing up to 1,000 feet covered with gorse and heath and with bracken and small oaks in the shallow valleys.

2. *The Northern Heather Moorland.* These are high undulating uplands rising to 1,400 feet where heather grows in profusion on the shallow peat. In the valleys you'll find bracken, gorse and the lovely rowans ablaze with red berries in autumn.

3. *The Central Grass Moors* where grow purple moor grass, deer sedge and cotton grass. In the few valleys rushes and matgrass can be found.

4. *The Southern Heather Moorland.* Here the main vegetation is heather but of all the regions of Exmoor this was the one that has been "reclaimed" more than any other and the natural vegetation has given way to enclosed land swamped with chemicals to produce the vegetation that man requires to farm here.

5. *Brendon Heaths.* There are a few areas of isolated heather and gorse uplands with bracken-filled valleys but much of the area has been covered with conifers. Man again changing the landscape.

Finally let me give you a few more names of plants and flowers that you might find on Exmoor. If this subject really interests you then there are excellent books given in the bibliography at the end of this guide that will help you identify the 900 or more different species that can be found!

The northern cliffs have a range of coastal flowers and plants that make it a delight to have such an area within a national park that is otherwise mainly moorland. Here you will find seapink and white sea campion and even the rare silver ragwort which grows in the areas of red sandstone. Right down on the coast on the shingle bank of Porlock Bay everlasting pea and yellow horned poppy thrive and of course salt loving plants such as seabeet and saltwort can be found on the marsh here. With many drainage ditches in this area you can expect burr marigold, yellow flag and other water loving plants.

On the drier moors you will find bell heather and ling as well as the heaths such as bedstraw, cross-leaved and milkwort. Lousewort and tormentil grow here and of course wortleberry or bilberry with its delicious, small, deep mauve berry that is so good to eat raw or make into pies and to be eaten with clotted cream!

On the high, peaty grass moors mentioned above you will also find common sedge and the lovely bog asphodel and if you are lucky the heath spotted orchid.

Along the rocky, wooded valleys you are likely to come across damp and shade loving ferns such as hard fern, common and black spleenwort and hartstongue. What marvellous names they are! Growing between the rocks and in walls you can see great woodrush, wall pennywort and cow wheat.

As you might expect the wet boggy places produce a mass of flowers such as bog pimpernel, marsh violet, lesser spearwort and marsh St John's wort. The lists could go on for ever with, as I said, over 900 to mention! It is a fascinating thing to watch as you walk and, even if you do not know what they are, to make a mental note of the incredible number of different varieties of plants, flowers, ferns, mosses, rushes and lichens that you will pass over in just a few miles.

Fauna

IN MY INTRODUCTION I mentioned some of the animals and birds that you will probably come across on Exmoor. As with Dartmoor the buzzard, wheeling round with its mewing cry, like a kitten, high above the edge of the woods that fill the combes and push towards the open moor, brings back a flood of happy memories of warm summer days and a deep sense of solitude with huge landscapes and skies. I always love the way buzzards side-slip about the sky with such disdain when evading the mobbing crows!

Kestrels and sparrow-hawks are the other most common birds of prey that you will see hovering or swooping over some luckless vole or mouse. If you watch closely you will see that the kestrel's head stays absolutely still even though its body, supported by the pulsating wings, may be twisting and turning to keep balance in the wind. This is to make sure that its eyes are also kept still because of their power of magnification and the intense concentration needed to follow every move of the prey.

Croaking ravens, curlews with their bubbling, evocative call and lapwings all frequent the high moor. Also on the higher moor, the wheatear starts to arrive in March from Africa to breed here; in Victorian times these small birds were considered a delicacy on many dinner tables.

Whinchats, ring ouzels, tree pipits and the willow warbler with its glorious, wistful song of gently descending notes can all be seen and heard in early April and June.

By the rivers, the dipper, that remarkable little, black and white bird that seems to fly underwater and builds its nests on overhanging rocks just above flood level, darts along with flitting flight, low over the water.

Also near the rivers you will often find chiff-chaffs, wagtails and that delightful small bird, the redstart. And you may disturb an old, grey heron fishing in the streams and lakes and off he'll go with long, languid flaps of his great wings. Even when frightened I have never seen herons speed up their wingbeats.

Then, because Exmoor comes to the edge of the sea in the north, you have the added attraction and fascination of watching out for seabirds when on your walks there. Gulls, guillemots and razorbills are the most common that you will find.

The wily, moorland fox has cousins that come scavenging in some of the small towns near Exmoor; the new breed of urban fox. If you are very fortunate you may come across badgers at dusk frolicking near their setts with their cubs or with even greater luck you might find the shy, almost extinct otter by the rippling streams and rivers, that writhing, graceful creature that we have almost killed off. If you do see them, keep quiet, don't tell a soul. Keep it as a secret to treasure all your life. They may not be here much longer. It is undisturbed peace they need to survive.

A vast number of insects are found on and around the moor including honey bees, dragonflies and spiders while butterflies and caterpillars including the emperor moth catch the eye with their bright colours.

Man has grazed his animals on Exmoor from the time of the Bronze Age and the moorland farmers still use the high moor. You'll see Exmoor horn and Cheviots as well as the ubiquitous Scottish blackface sheep here and Galloway and black Welsh hill cattle, all creatures that can survive on the bleak, open moor.

I have already mentioned the Exmoor ponies. Although people say they are wild they are all owned by local farmers and breeders. Though there are many cross-breeds, the true-bred Exmoors are all descended from the Anchor herd of Ashway Farm that were kept to keep the breed pure when Exmoor Forest was sold off to private buyers. The park authority has now also taken on this responsibility by running two herds of pure-bred ponies which it started in 1980. Like the sheep and cattle they have to be able to stand up to the hardships of living on the moor with a thick coat to keep out the wind and rain. They exist on the grasses, heathers and bracken

Exmoor pony

found on Exmoor.

However I cannot end a section on the animals of Exmoor without mention of "The Beast"!

During the various occasions that I have been on expeditions in the Himalayas I have always been fascinated by tales of the Yeti and I have had many happy hours talking to the Sherpas about this mysterious creature. As I am a romantic by nature I like to believe that such a beast exists and it is the same for me, with "The Beast of Exmoor."

What are the facts? Well, ever since the early 1980s there have been reports from all over Exmoor of lambs, ewes, even deer and a foal being discovered horribly mutilated and half eaten. Stories, too, of terrible screams being heard in the night! There were sightings as well, with usually the same description - a large black cat-like creature with wild staring eyes!

The police were called in, as were the marines with special snipers and night viewing equipment. The R.A.F. provided a helicopter, local farmers set up a vigilante group to watch their flocks, national newspapers offered rewards for a photograph, all to no avail.

The reports kept coming in of killings and always with the same description: a sort of large, black cat with fierce, green eyes and a long tail. Huge footprints were photographed suggesting a creature of up to 150lbs. So what was it, or is it? A black panther, a puma, a lynx that might have escaped from a small zoo or wildlife park or perhaps a dog that had gone wild and was living by hunting? Who knows. All has been quiet now for a couple of years but I expect "The Beast of Exmoor" to strike again any day now, so keep an eye out when you are out alone in the wild and lonely spots of the moor!

The Red Deer

THIS GUIDEBOOK is no place to enter into the strongly felt controversies and passions surrounding stag-hunting on Exmoor and the Quantocks. I must not take sides but I feel that I should air a few points that, to me, seem important.

There is no argument against the hard fact that the deer on Exmoor and the Quantocks must be culled if they are to survive as a wild breed. If they are not, lack of fodder would starve many to death as the herds increased in number. Poachers would move in indiscriminately and angry farmers would slaughter all deer on sight, for they do fearful damage to crops. The problem is to know which is the best, most humane and efficient method to carry out this culling; is it to be hunting or shooting? The arguments will rage forever about that with wild and usually inaccurate accusations coming from both sides.

Stag-hunting is an old and important part of the country life of Exmoor where it is not just the sport of the rich and leisured minority. Many of the local farmers are keen members of the hunt and a meet brings out hundred of foot and car followers. There are also many other country businesses, occupations and events in the area that are directly or indirectly connected with stag-hunting that would probably decline and vanish if the deer were no longer to roam the moors and woods of Exmoor.

What about the animal itself? The stags are the most noble and magnificent of creatures; the kings of all our British mammals, with a direct link back to their prehistoric past. They stand nearly four feet at the shoulder and when the antlers are fully developed they may well top six feet. The hinds are smaller by some six inches and have no antlers.

Their coats are a ruddy-brown in colour and, like the ponies, are thick enough to keep them warm in the bleak, cold winter months. Both the stags and the hinds have large but well shaped ears to cup the smallest sounds, for their hearing is acute. By the same token their sense of smell is well developed for it is on both of these senses that they depend for their safety.

It is the antlers of the stags that are their most remarkable feature and give them their royal appearance. They shed and renew them every year and it takes only some sixteen weeks for them to gain their full majesty; one of nature's extraordinary feats. As they start to grow, the tender horns are covered with a protective skin called the velvet which is rubbed off as the antlers develop.

The hinds usually mate in their second year and after eight months the calves are born in June in thick woodland. These lovely, little creatures are delightful with long legs and dappled coats; pure Walt Disney Bambis! In the early days of their lives they cannot run with the herd and the hind will push the vulnerable calf into cover if there is danger, which is announced by a sharp bark and a stamp of the forefoot. Here it will lie motionless until she can return, sometimes having even drawn the danger away herself. Also at night the calf will rest in cover while his mother feeds until she arrives back with a gentle bark and much nuzzling of her youngster.

The deer of Exmoor move about usually in herds of up to 30 but I have seen small groups of only three and four that may have been separated from others. They usually move in single file with the stags rounding up the hinds from the rear. There are probably some 800 red deer on Exmoor. The numbers in the Quantocks have fallen because of poaching.

With man their only enemy, they are shy creatures and you will be lucky to see them on your first visit to Exmoor. They prefer the old oak woods in the steep-sided valleys that open out onto moor where they can graze at night moving back into the covets by day. You might be lucky to find them above Horner Water, Hawkcombe, Culbone Woods or near Badgworthy but they could be anywhere and even the trained stag harbourer can be wrong.

When October arrives it is the rutting or mating season which lasts about a month. It is then that the stags round up as many hinds with their young calves as they can control, and become extremely aggressive not only to other stags but even towards humans. They rip at the ground with their antlers, gouge banks with their hooves and charge at small bushes and trees. If they are challenged by other stags they will enter combat sometimes even to death. They meet head on with antlers locked and, with tremendous straining and twisting, try to force the opponent to lower his guard. Sooner or later one will admit defeat and try to disengage their antlers and swing away. It is then that a fatal wound can be delivered in the flank of the retreating stag.

One of the other extraordinary signs of aggression the stag will show during the rut is what is called belling. It is a weird, hair-prickling sound and is a strange mixture between "a bellow and a roar that ends with a coughing grunt!" If you have ever heard it you will never forget the sound, especially if it is at night!

The stag was once perhaps glibly called "the monarch of the glen" but I can find no better description and it is always with delight, enchantment and humbleness that I see red deer on Exmoor; the lords of life.

Man on Exmoor
EVIDENCE ABOUT the occupation of Exmoor by man in the very early prehistoric times is limited and vague. Tiny flint arrow heads and other tools such as scrapers have been found and these have been identified as probably coming from the Mesolithic or Middle Stone Age. At Hawkcombe Head there were enough of these flints found to suggest a knapping floor but beyond that there is nothing to prove that man actually lived on Exmoor, so he probably wandered up into the area on hunting trips killing animals for their skins to make clothing and shelters.

By 5000 B.C. the people we call the New Stone Age had arrived, probably from Asia Minor, migrating and looking for new areas to settle in. These Neolithic men were really quite advanced in comparison with the Mesolithic people. They made pottery and, because they had discovered ploughing, they grew corn and even kept cattle, sheep and pigs. They were still hunters and they also used flint arrow heads and knives. Their polished stone axes were capable of felling trees. Again there is no hard evidence that they actually settled and lived on Exmoor but the round barrow at Easter New Moor might have been made by them. The earthern ring near Parracombe could also have been a meeting place or henge for the New Stone Age tribes.

I suppose that the discovery and the use of metal marks one of the most important developments and stepping stones in the history of man. By 3000 B.C. new tribes had arrived from Europe bringing with them their knowledge of the use of copper and tin that resulted in what we call the Bronze Age. Indeed it might have been the fact that copper was found on Exmoor and tin farther south and west that attracted these people here. They seemed to have overlapped happily with the Neolithic people and we can see evidence of the old skills and ways of life mixing with the new. Warring and fighting between tribes does not seem to have occurred. They were still farmers and hunters and by now the women probably spun and wove. Highly respected, I am sure, were the bronze-smiths, skilled craftsmen who produced not only the everyday implements for their lives but the most beautiful cups, pommels of daggers, necklaces and jewellery.

It is with the Bronze Age that we have the first hard evidence that man lived on Exmoor. There are traces of their farming, ruins of their circular huts and of course you will find the burial mounds, the round barrows, the mysterious standing stones and stone rows. While these are numerous, I have to admit the area is not quite as impressive or so rich in Bronze Age remains as Dartmoor, though they make interesting objectives for some of the walks.

By 500 B.C. man had discovered iron and the Celts brought this to Britain when they came. They also seemed happy to settle with the people whom they found here but not so the Gauls who followed them. They were a warlike nation that set about conquering the inhabitants and then waging war against each other!

It was these people, the Celts and Gauls with their druids and superstitious rites that Julius Caesar found when he invaded in 55 BC. living a life of quite prosperous farming. But as Caesar himself tells, they were aggressive fighters not only against his forces but against each other. It is no wonder that there are many hill forts from this period, five of which can be found on or near Exmoor. The most exciting find from this, the Iron Age, was a really beautiful bronze bowl from Munson farm, Rose Ash, now in the British Museum.

When the Romans finally came to Britain in A.D. 43 they had little influence on the life and people of Exmoor. There are the remains of the two small forts on the north coast at Martinhoe and Old Burrow but for the most part they stayed farther south, at Exeter.

The fifth and sixth centuries brought the invasion of Britain by the Angles and Saxons and of course the legends of Arthur. On Exmoor all we have is the sixth century Latin inscription on the Caratacus Stone on Winsford Hill.

Christianity had also arrived by now and missionaries from Ireland and Wales came across the Irish Sea and Bristol Channel to land on the coasts of Exmoor and this is reflected in the names of some of the churches and villages here; St Petrock, St Beuno and St Brendan are just a few.

It was about this time that the Harepath (a Saxon word meaning army road) became important. This prehistoric track can still be traced on Exmoor and was the means of allowing large bodies of men and equipment to move quickly from one area to another. It ran from the Midlands to Bristol and over the Somerset levels to the Quantocks. From there it crossed the Brendons to Exmoor and finally to Cornwall. Some of the walks cross or come near the Harepath.

These were the Dark Ages when the whole history of Britain, let alone Exmoor, was shrouded in doubt and mystery. Little snippets emerge here and there until we come to times that are within our own recorded writings and memories.

The Domesday Book lets us know something of what life was like in 1086 on Exmoor. The land was divided into manors which were quite large, thriving farms with land for ploughing and grazing where they kept sheep, oxen and goats. Often around the main farm were huts where the serfs and villeins lived. How those names bring back the memory of distant history lessons! It is here that the wild ponies of Exmoor are first mentioned; *"equas indomitas and equas silvestres"*. It is also at this time that the commoners' rights were established with the high moor being used for grazing and peat cutting.

With the Normans the power of the kings became greater and as with Dartmoor we now have the establishment of what was called the Forest of Exmoor. This did not mean that Exmoor was an area of trees and woodland but that it was a royal hunting ground. The other interesting legacy of the Normans was the building of castles close to Exmoor at Bury Castle near Dulverton, Holwell Castle, Parracombe, and Stowey Castle at Nether Stowey.

With such a large area to look after and control, the post of Warden of the Forest was created. This hereditary title probably dates from 1066 but was well established by 1204. For a while Edward IV himself took on the title and the responsibility. In 1300 there was a perambulation that fixed boundaries of the lands of the forest belonging to the King. I shall be giving the details of this as one of the walks later on in this book. After 1508 the wardens not only looked after the administration of the forest but they also leased the land from the kings.

The wardens in their turn appointed foresters who acted as gamekeepers and drovers. Often they were paid no wages and in some cases were charged for the privilege of being a forester and were quite obviously a kind of Exmoor mafia gaining a living by blackmail and extortion of the luckless people who had settled in the forest and were trying to exist farming there. The foresters would impound their cattle, sheep and ponies or bring false charges under the Forest Law and then demand payment. This seemed to have been the way of life until the sale of the Forest in 1818. Those of you who wish to find out more about this subject will find several books, the best known by G.T.Turner of 1901.

One of the most interesting and remarkable of the wardens was James Boevey. Boevey was a wealthy merchant of Dutch ancestry who, at the age of 32, gave up city life and trading and retired to the country. He was able to purchase the freehold of Exmoor in 1651 as "The Commons of England assembled in Parliament" passed an act for the sale of lands belonging to the late King (Charles I), Queen and Prince.

John Aubrey writes about him in his *Brief Lives* and Boevey appears to have been an extraordinarily active man. He wrote 32 books and spoke eight languages. Aubrey says that, "From 14 he had a candle burning by him all night, with pen, inke and paper, to write downe thoughts as they came into his head; so that he might not lose

James Boevey's and the Knight's House at Simonsbath

a thought". He seems to have spent most of his life engaged in litigation against the commoners or the rights of the Free Suitors and making, as you might expect, many enemies along that road. His increase in the demands for payment for grazing within the lands he now owned brought an outcry from local farmers who retaliated by boycotting the pastures. This might have been a set-back for him but by crafty negotiations he was able eventually to get a court settlement that enabled him to set the rates for grazing at whatever level he wished.

In 1654 James Boevey built and then lived at Simonsbath House which still stands today, used as a hotel. Another reminder of James Boevey is the Hoar Oak Tree. This famous landmark, visited on some of the walks that follow, was reported in 1658 to have fallen down "with very age and rottenness". How long before that it had been known is not certain, but it was one of the boundary markers of the perambulation of the Forest of Exmoor. So in 1662 James Boevey in a fit of patriotic zeal towards Charles II, planted another Hoar Oak. Charles, of course, had hidden in an oak tree after the Battle of Worcester and it had become a symbol of his escape. All those pubs called the Royal Oak are named for the same reason!

But in January 1696 James Boevey died after 43 tempestuous years as Warden of the Forest. His third wife took over and became only the second woman to be a warden of Exmoor, but she lacked her husband's zest for squabbles and gave up after eight years and sold her lease to one Robert Siderfin. There were others to follow such as the three generations of Sir Thomas Dyke Acland who did much for the wildlife on Exmoor, especially the deer and ponies. They held the office until the lease from the crown expired in 1814.

It was at this time, as mentioned earlier, that the suggestion by the crown surveyor, a Mr Richard Hawkins, that high Exmoor could be used for growing oaks and other trees for making wooden ships was put forward. This scheme was partly responsible for the momentous changes that were to take place from then on. The result was that the crown decided to enclose and divide the forest rather than lease it as before. To further this scheme an Act of Inclosure was passed in 1815. It seems odd that Mr Hawkins who had passed the stunted Hoar Oak Tree on the last perambulation of the Forest of Exmoor in 1815 should still be advising the crown that oaks would grow on the high moor! In any case the inclosure commissioners alloted over 10,000 acres to the king, some 3,000 acres to Sir Thomas Acland and just under 2,000 acres to a Sir Charles Bamfylde. They also arranged for the Free Suitors and the Suitors at Large to be awarded small allotments of 31 acres in lieu of their ancient grazing rights; as you might expect, this was far too small to eke out a fair living, and many sold their land to the rich.

By 1818 the commissioners of woods and forests had come to their senses and realised that it was quite impossible to grow trees, let alone oaks, on Exmoor and put the 10,000 acres of the king's land up for sale by tender, as no fortune was to be made there.

There now arrived on the scene the family that was to influence and instigate many of the profound changes that were to have a lasting effect; the Knights of Exmoor.

They were not from Exmoor originally but from Shropshire and Worcestershire where they had been prosperous ironmasters for generations, back to Cromwellian times. John Knight put in a tender of £50,000 (a lot of money in those days) for the king's lands. As it was the highest of the seven tenders submitted, the allotment, as it was quaintly called, went to John Knight as reported in *The Taunton Courier:* "The property is near Simond's Bath; the greater part to be inclosed by a wall, in the centre of which a handsome residence is to be built. The spot affords great facilities for this purpose, and will under the judicious plans in contemplation become an enviable possession."

So really a thousand years of the Royal Forest of Exmoor had come to an end, but a new era had begun, for indeed John Knight had "judicious plans". His family had always faced up to challenges and adventure in the development of their foundries and here was new endeavour to be found by tackling and taming the wilderness of Exmoor and making something of it by struggle and hard work. But behind it was also a vision, for they were aware that it was essential to make agriculture more efficient and land use more productive with the rapidly developing attitudes of the early years of that century. The venture would attract huge risks but also much would be gained, not just in monetary terms. There must have been a lot of pride, too, in taking over land that had belonged to the crown for hundreds of years, not to mention the social status it would bring, for it was the great landowners who still ruled much of England.

So, as he must have told the reporters from *The Taunton Courier,* John Knight built his wall round the estate; some 29 miles of it. You will still find traces of it near Black Barrow and Badgworthy and on to Brendon. The building of this wall was not at all popular with the Suitors at Large for many of them thought that John Knight was going to enclose and take away their grazing on the Brendons as well. It is said that the lengths of wall that were constructed during the day by John Knight's workers were knocked down at night by the men of Brendon!

Knight settled at Simonsbath, with his family as he promised, in James Boevey's old house and, because the roads in the area were appalling, he set about making new roads as well, some 22 miles of them.

He had plans for a Great House to be built behind the existing Simonsbath House, but it was never completed though the empty shell could be seen until it was pulled down in 1899.

Employing some 200 Irish labourers he built a dam across the upper reaches of the Barle and created a lake now called Pinkworthy Pond. Why he did this is not certain but in any case it still makes a pleasant sight on the edge of the high moor.

He was determined to make the farming on Exmoor prosper and though he still let out the grazing, he set about draining, ploughing and liming much of the peaty land to create over 2500 acres of ground for wheat and barley.

Although he did not have much success with his arable land he did do well with stock-rearing and was responsible for introducing Hereford and West Highland cattle and crossing Cheviots with the Exmoor breeds of sheep. He also tried to introduce Arab stallions to the Exmoor mares but despite all his efforts and struggles it seems as if Exmoor and its harsh, wet climate and severe winters had the final say. None of these experiments could be said to be an outstanding success, though the battle went on.

By 1840 perhaps his desire for challenge was fading a little and John Knight handed over the running of his Exmoor estates to his son Frederic. In spite of retiring to Rome in 1842 he kept in constant touch with the life on Exmoor and showed deep concern for its development. He died in Rome in 1850.

Frederic had learnt from his father's courageous efforts and realised that Exmoor needed to have more people living and farming there and helping with the improvements needed. He built farms for tenant farmers and protected both the buildings and the fields by planting long wind-breaks of beeches, still one of the outstanding features of Exmoor today. He made sure that there was a school and a church, the hubs of village life, at Simonsbath.

He gave up his father's idea of growing cereals and concentrated on sheep. To gain better grazing he planted rape crops with grass seeds and the now permanent pastures for his sheep flourished with a team of Scottish shepherds to look after more than 5,000 animals.

The dream of handing on, as an inheritance, his lands and the Knight way of life was cruelly thwarted when his only son died in 1879 aged 28. Sir Frederic, who never really got over his grief, was knighted for his services to the public, and he himself died in 1897 still intensely interested in farming his 9,000 acres, with a sheep for every acre, grazing on his land. The Forest of Exmoor was as

Ruins of the winding house at the top of the Incline on the Brendons

populated and as flourishing as it had ever been. The Knight family had found their challenge and had brought an ambition to reality. They had found a way to farm Exmoor commercially and by example and help had encouraged others to make their livings on the high moor. They had changed not only attitudes but also the landscape of Exmoor itself and present-day farmers still owe much to the Knights for showing them the ways and the means to tame the harsh land and eke out an existence.

One other way that man has left his mark on Exmoor is through his mining activities. Iron ore was found here but who started mining for it is not certain. Some say the Romans, but there is no proof of this. Similarly, in 1550 Michael Wynston was known to have had a licence to dig for iron ore but again no real details have emerged. We have to look at the 1830s to find hard and fast evidence of mining at Chargot near Luxborough, albeit only a small industry. However, as the ore was rich - containing some 60% iron - it attracted the attention of a Welsh entrepreneur, Ebenezer Rogers, and so started the Brendon Hill Iron Ore Company.

There is a saying that at the bottom of every hole you will find a

Cornish miner. In the Brendon mines you would have found not only Cornish but also Welsh and North Country miners. They sank 31 shafts and over the years they brought out some 750,000 tons of iron ore. Little mining communities were built at Gupworthy and other places and with so many Cornish and Welsh inhabitants, so were chapels. What singing must have echoed over the Brendon Hills! All around were the stores, winding gear houses and engine sheds. Most remarkable of all was the mineral line railway. The ore had to be shipped to Barry in South Wales and the port they used was Watchet on the Bristol Channel. The problem was how to get the ore from a height of 1,200 feet on the Brendons down to Watchet for, although you could almost see the town from the mines, no horse-drawn carts could cope with both the large quantities of ore being produced or the steep slopes involved. Nor indeed could a steam railway be used to link the two directly, again because of the gradient.

Not to be thwarted, the mining company set about building first, six miles of easy gradient railway line to the foot of the escarpment on the north side of the Brendon Hills. They then hacked, blasted and hewed their way to the top creating an amazing incline a mile long with a one-in-four gradient. One of the walks investigates this quite incredible engineering feat. From the top there were rail links to the mines and on through to the terminus at Gupworthy. You can still find the remains of the line running through the cuttings, along embankments that must have been flanked by the spoil tips, engine houses and all the other clutter of a thriving, busy mining industry; all is full of ghosts now.

The incline itself worked by gravity with the descending full ore truck pulling the empty one to the top, all controlled by an eighteen foot drum with steel cables round it and a winding engine and a braking system. What remarkable people these Victorians were!

There were other mines near Heasley Mill and Tabor Hill. They produced mainly copper but also iron ore and even silver and gold. The Wheal Eliza mine just south of Simonsbath had a long adit and a shaft over 300 feet deep. Frederic Knight became involved in this development but as always the problems of getting the ore away by building a railway proved too much financially and in any case the yield of ore was poor and the project failed. Another walk will take you to look at the remains there and then I shall be able to recount one of the rather more gruesome stories of Exmoor!

Finally, all around there is evidence of farming on Exmoor from early times to the modern, hard-headed farmer who is being encouraged to diversify in these difficult days. Exmoor is still a hard task-master for these hill-farmers and it is no easy "feather-bed" life to maintain an existence on the moor by stock-rearing and grazing. You will see their Galloways and Herefords and the French Charolais. The breeds that the Knights introduced are still here amongst the sheep; Cheviots mixing with the Exmoor horns and Scotch blackfaces.

The Legends of Exmoor

BECAUSE MAN HAS lived on Exmoor since prehistoric times and as the landscape itself is so often weird and mysterious, it is no wonder that there are many legends and folk tales in the area. Some of them, of course, are founded on truth with real characters, but others try to give a reason for some strange happening or offer an explanation of an unaccountable occurrence for simple, superstitious people. I must say that there have been quite a few times while walking on Exmoor when I have had an inexplicable prickling at the back of my neck, sometimes on the Harepath or near some of the old burial grounds and have been aware of some mysterious presence!

As might be expected quite a number of the stories are linked with the Devil. There is one theory that he heaped up Dunkery Beacon with one huge spadeful of rock to leave the hollow near Winsford known as the Devil's Punchbowl!

On one of the walks you will visit Tarr Steps and when you do, keep an eye out for the Devil, for he actually built the famous clapper bridge and can be found sunbathing there and could well demand your soul and more if you try to cross! There is a lovely story told of how some local people sent a cat across one day to see if the Devil was about. When the cat disappeared with a flash and a puff of sulphurous smoke they knew he must be there! They then persuaded their parson to try to get rid of him! The Devil, meeting the parson in the middle of the bridge, bombarded him with a flow of foul language that wilted all the trees in Hatt Wood. But this particular cleric knew a thing or two and, having mixed with

Pony Trekkers

Exmoor Cottages

Exmoor farming folk, I am sure returned the vulgar tirade with a far more extensive vocabulary of expletives than the Devil had ever heard before! He was so taken aback that he agreed that people could cross the steps unless he was sunbathing!

There are enough legends and ghost stories to almost fill this book: King Arthur and the sea-serpent, St Decuman arriving from Wales on a hurdle, Florence Wyndham rising from the dead, Mother Shipton, the whistling ghost of Mistress Leakey, The naked boy, The white dove of Bardon - I shall come back to some of these during the descriptions of the walks.

Then there are smugglers' tales, highwaymen's exploits and what about pixies?

The king of the pixies was supposed to have lived at Knighton Farm near Withypool and ruled over the small people. They lived in tiny, turf-covered huts and knew all the secret ways through the forests, bogs and marshes. They could melt away into the wild moor carrying with them stolen cattle, children and kidnapped womenfolk. They were also responsible for all kinds of tricks and practical jokes such as leading men astray up the wrong roads when coming home late from market (were the pubs still open I hear you ask?!), steal horses to have races, make people dance all night in their fairy rings. So don't go up into the wild combe between Challacombe and Chapman's Barrows, for although I have written in the past tense about the pixies, you never can tell! Marwood de Winchelhalse in *Lorna Doone* says, "No dog, no man, is rule about here when it comes to coppice work; there is not a man who dare work here without a dog to scare the pixies".

At last the name of Lorna Doone has cropped up! You probably thought that I would never get round to it! Was it true, and if so how much of it was? Was it all fiction or half and half? I am not going into a long, literary essay, about the locations Blackmore used and whether the book was based on truth or legend. All I can say is, read *Lorna Doone* yourself, if you haven't already done so as a youngster at school and see what you think. It is a fine book and gives a marvellous picture of Exmoor and possibly something of Exmoor life at that time. I shall obviously refer to certain parts of the book

Porlock Weir with Bossington Hill in the background

when describing the walk down the Doone valley or a visit to some of the places used by Blackmore, but beyond that I shall not go, for plenty of others have done just that and you will find the bookshops full of their efforts!

Exmoor Today

EXMOOR WAS established as a national park in 1954. It is, in fact, the second smallest national park in England and Wales covering only some 265 square miles of which roughly one third is in Devon and two-thirds in Somerset. Only the Pembrokeshire Coast national park is smaller.

Exmoor, because it is so small, is particularly vulnerable to modern pressures. The pressures are enormous from walkers and other tourists. It is, of course, not just the tourists that cause the problems. Many other seemingly conflicting interests such as farming, forestry and small industries all make the work of conserving the area extremely difficult.

Clearly as the horrors of urban life build up, more and more people will escape into the quiet and peace of the countryside - but do they really want that? I sometimes doubt it when I see the crowded car parks, traffic jams in the narrow lanes, lovely picnic sites looking like Blackpool Beach, loud with blaring radios and ankle-deep in litter. By coming to Exmoor in their hordes they destroy the very thing they think they are looking for.

So there has to be control, discipline, money and understanding care to make sure that Exmoor still retains its beauty and wildness without, on the one hand, stifling and thwarting those who have to make a living on the moor or, on the other, making the National Park like some awful, sterile exhibit with tight controls including permission of entry and with concrete paths to walk on such as you find in some American parks.

For so many to come to Exmoor - and the number of visitors each year is fast approaching three million - means that in many cases they have to be educated gently as to how to use the countryside including the open moorland, which many regard as land not owned by anybody. This, in fact, is not true. The Exmoor National Park does not belong to the nation as the name implies; it is all owned by the farmers and other landowners including those who have the grazing rights. Luckily the Exmoor National Park Authority also has large holdings of moorland and fields and some 800 acres of grazing rights at Larkbarrow.

To start protecting this heritage you could find no better advice than the Country Code:

1. Guard against all risk of fire.
2. Fasten all gates.
3. Keep dogs under proper control.
4. Keep to paths across farmland and then only if there is a right of way.
5. Avoid damaging fences, hedges, wall and gates - particularly by climbing over them.
6. Leave no litter - take it home.
7. Safeguard water supplies.
8. Protect wildlife, wild plants and trees.
9. Drive and walk carefully on narrow country roads. (It is important to know how to back your car and be prepared to do so!)
10. Respect the life of the countryside and those who live there.

Coupled with this last one I should like to add another.

11. Do not make unnecessary noise.

I should also mention the notices put up at many places stating that there should be, "No Vehicles beyond this point". This is not a national park law but a highway law that states that no vehicles can be driven more than 15 yards from a road. Following on from this I would urge all car users to park sensibly and with consideration. Do not block gates as local farmers and other users of the moor need to come and go without hindrance. Do not park in narrow lanes or on busy roads.

Access can also cause problems. No wonder many Exmoor farmers still regard the tourist as a scourge. I have seen people tramping across a fine crop of hay to have a picnic. All too often groups will climb over walls and fences to cut off a corner. I have seen dogs completely out of control chasing and yapping at sheep and cattle. I have heard farmers complaining of gates left open to allow their animals to wander onto the roads or to stray into fields where they should not go. We have all found empty tin cans and broken bottles left around; a terrible danger to livestock. Cigarette packets and butt ends, fish and chip papers, crisp packets and fried chicken cartons all litter popular areas of the moor and are often blown or thrown onto private land.

The public footpaths and bridle-paths are clearly marked on the maps you will be using. Many of them are also waymarked with posts and boards; too many maybe, as I mentioned earlier. Please stick to and respect the rights of way and do not stray off them. As a good, general rule you can assume that all enclosed fields are private and that you should not enter them unless there is a marked right of way either on the map or by a sign.

If you have any doubts or queries about anything to do with the area, the Exmoor National Park Centre, Exmoor House, Dulverton, Somerset. TA22 9HL Tel: Dulverton (0398) 23665 are always happy to help and advise. There are also several seasonal information centres at strategic places on the moor including Exmoor House, Dunster Steep Car Park, The Esplanade, Lynmouth, Combe Martin and the County Gate on the A39 between Porlock and Lynmouth. You will also see, going about their work, quite a number of park rangers, who amongst their many jobs, act as a liaison with the public.

The Exmoor National Park Authority does a splendid but extremely difficult job of trying to hold that delicate balance between being aware that Exmoor is a living, vibrant eco-system that needs protecting and nurturing and yet allowing development and use that respects this.

The environment is not infinitely self-restoring. Damage is mostly the result of ignorance, thoughtlessness or carelessness. Man is part of this eco-system and his awareness of the problems and how to preserve and conserve it, and how to develop care and concern, should not give rise to restriction but freedom with responsibility. The Exmoor National Park Authority does all it can, with limited resources and, of course, lack of proper finances, to help us carry out our responsibilities.

Where to Stay

AS YOU DRIVE across or around Exmoor you will often see farms and small guest houses advertising bed and breakfast. This is a marvellous way to get to know an area for, particularly with farmhouse B&B, the local people will be only too glad to give you advice and information about the area. You may be the sort of person who likes to try places on the off-chance that they will have vacancies, but at the peak holiday periods you would probably be better off booking.

Exmoor is famous for its many excellent hotels ranging from the large and expensive to the small and not so expensive. Many offer special facilities such as fishing, riding and walking. The national park authority publishes a newspaper called *The Exmoor Visitor* that lists many B&B's, guest houses and hotels. There are youth hostels at Dunster, Lynbridge and Exford. Tourist information centres like those at Minehead, Lynmouth and Combe Martin will try to find you accommodation and even book ahead if your destination is in their area. There is a small charge for this.

As I have mentioned, all Exmoor is privately owned and per-mission must be obtained from landowners before pitching tents or caravans. Some farmers will allow you to camp on their land for short periods. There are, however, quite a number of recognised and registered camp sites for both tents and caravans and some are on farms. *The Exmoor Visitor* gives you further details about camp-ing and also lists of the various sites on or near Exmoor.

Exmoor Weather

AS WITH MANY upland regions in the west of Britain you can expect a high rainfall on Exmoor, except along the coastal area and the Vale of Porlock. The prevailing westerly winds come in from the Atlantic loaded with moisture and, lying as it does on the peninsula with the English Channel on one side and the Irish Sea and the Bristol Channel on the other, the average rainfall of nearly eighty inches near Chains Barrow and Winsford is to be expected. Sur-prisingly perhaps, this average drops to only 35 inches on the coast where it is almost in a "rain shadow" with most of the water having fallen on the moor behind.

This oceanic climate coupled with the fact that a lot of Exmoor is between 200 and 400 metres high means that there will be ferocious winds as well as heavy rain and the notorious mists that can blow up in minutes. Good weather proof gear is necessary to combat such weather, along with a decent pair of light-weight walking boots and, in the rucksack, emergency food and first aid equipment. All walkers on Exmoor, especially on the higher, open moorland regions, must be prepared both physically and mentally for mist as well as violent driving storms of wind and rain. In winter there are often hard frosts and snow with deep drifts driven by the wind. Extra clothing is necessary at such times.

You can telephone for recorded weather forecasts for Exmoor on; 0898 141203. They are quite expensive but are updated three times a day.

One final word about flooded streams and rivers. Exmoor is like a great sponge which retains water until saturation point is reached and then it releases huge quantities with amazing suddenness. You will have heard, I am sure, of the terrible flood which struck Lynmouth in 1952. The rivers can come up several feet within an hour or less. The power and weight of water of a river in flood is something that you would never imagine unless you try to cross. The rule is - don't! It is far better to walk an extra mile or more to an easier crossing place or a bridge rather than attempt to wade across, especially with young people. Hopping from boulder to boulder is also to be discouraged at all times, even more so with a river in spate; it usually ends with wet clothing or worse, a sprained ankle or broken bone. If you have a light rope with you then, in a real emergency, you might feel that it was vital to cross using one of the safe-guarding methods shown in Langmuir's book mentioned in the Bibliography.

Maps & Compass

THE MOST POPULAR map of Exmoor used to be the one inch to the mile (1:63360) tourist map which contains the whole moor on the one map and extends westward as far as Bideford and south to North Tawton and east to include most of the Brendon Hills. It is ideal for driving round within the area. With the move to metric maps the ones that are now available are the Landranger Series of

Great Britain which are based on a scale of 2cm to 1km (1:50,000) or about 1¼ inches to the mile. You will need two sheets for the whole of Exmoor: Sheet 181, Minehead and the Brendon Hills area and Sheet 180, Barnstaple and Ilfracombe area.

The Ordnance Survey has not yet produced a map in its Outdoor Leisure Series for Exmoor, though I gather one is in preparation. The scale of these maps is 4cm to 1km (1:25,000) or 2½ inches to the mile. This is a marvellous scale for details as walls, buildings and small differences in terrain and height are seen much more easily and are a great help when navigating, especially in bad weather.

However, you can get individual sheets of the 1:25,000 maps in the Pathfinder Series of Great Britain. The only snag is that you will need eight sheets to cover Exmoor, the Brendons and the Quantocks. They are SS64/74, SS84/94, ST04/14, SS63/73, SS83/93, ST03/13, ST23/33, SS82/92, but they are well worth buying.
NB The walks described are based on these maps and various names may not appear on the 1:50,000 map.

There will be occasions when the moor is so featureless, or you are in thick mist or even at night, when you will not be able to navigate visually either by lining up features or walking towards known points identified both on the map and on the ground. It is then that you will have to rely on your compass by taking and using compass bearings.

An ability to use map and compass is essential in wild country and with this you should be able to find your way around Exmoor, but navigation is a complex, fascinating and satisfying subject and well worth following up. It is just as well to have more than one person in your party who is competent with a map and a compass.

One final bit of advice. I should get a good, large, waterproof map case or cover your map with a clear, plastic, self-adhesive sheet or maybe spray it with one of the waterproofing fluids that are available. Wet, windy days on Exmoor can quickly destroy a map!

Walking on Exmoor
ON THE HIGH open moor you could, if you wished, go in almost any direction you felt like but a lot of the walking on Exmoor is very awkward with thick heather clumps and grass tussocks. Along with

the many walls and fences you would be better off following tracks wherever possible. Once off the high open moor, you will have to follow the rights of way and the waymarked paths.

Both on my suggested walks and the ones that you may plan yourself, you might like to work on the formula known as Naismith's Rule for finding out how long it is going to take you. Naismith was a Scottish climber, who in 1892, suggested that people walk at three miles per hour and that they had to add half an hour for every 1,000 feet they climbed. In these days of metric maps this becomes five kilometres per hour plus half an hour for every 300 metres of ascent. This really is only a starting point because in bad weather, or if you are unfit or carrying a load, or if the terrain is difficult, then you must take all or some of these into consideration and it is important for you to work out your own rule accordingly for you and your party.

On the various tracks on Exmoor you will be able to make quite good time if you want to, but on the open moor, away from the tracks maybe, a lot of your walking will be over tussocks of grass, heather and bracken in the summer months as well as peat hags, marshy areas and gorse, all within a few miles of each other. Sometimes it is almost impossible to get into that slow, rhythmical, steady stride that will keep you going all day and is so important for easy walking. All the same, try to keep a steady pace and with luck you may be able to average two to two and a half miles per hour or three to four kilometres per hour. You should certainly allow at least ten minutes in every hour in your calculations to rest and look around you or to consult the map and certainly more if you wish to stop, look at and explore some of the points of interest that I shall be mentioning.

So plan the route with the help of this guide, if you wish. Work out approximately how long it is going to take you. Check the weather, by telephoning for a forecast or looking in a local paper (The *Western Morning News* has very good forecasts and weather maps) before you set out and then keep a weather eye out, as they say, while you are walking.

Solo walking is a most exhilarating and worthwhile thing to do but obviously it has its dangers. Ideally your party should be at least three in number, from a safety point of view, when out in poor conditions on high Exmoor. In the event of an accident, one can go for help, while the other stays with the injured or ill person. I hope that it will never happen to you but if you do find yourself in trouble on Exmoor with an injured person or if one of your party is suffering from hypothermia or if somebody is lost, you may have to call for rescue. To do this get down to a call-box or a farm or private house with a phone and ring 999 and ask to be put in touch with the police and they will mount a rescue. This is the normal procedure in all the mountainous areas of Britain when you need to call out a rescue team.

Some advice I most certainly would not give to people walking in the mountains in other parts of Britain but would be quite safe to use on Exmoor is to follow a stream or river down if you are really badly lost. It will take you off the moor to civilization and probably a telephone if needs be.

Finally it is wise to leave word with someone telling them where you are going and how long you reckon you will be. Better still leave a written route card with details of your walk and estimated times if you are going on a journey across the higher areas of Exmoor. If you live or are staying in a hotel away from the Exmoor area and just drive there to walk, it might be a good idea to leave a note on the windscreen of your car again with details of your route, with timings. But there is a terrible dilemma here which sadly sums up the age we live in. Such notes are an invitation for a thief to break into the car and steal any valuables you might foolishly have left, or worse still, steal your car. What a world!

Using the Guide
IN ORDER, I hope, to make using this guide as easy as possible I have grouped the walks into four areas of Exmoor with the Brendons and the Quantocks as two other additional sections. I have used the main roads as the boundaries, although it is not an entirely satisfactory method.

1. The North-west Moor. The boundary of the national park is the western edge of this area. The B3358 as far as Simonsbath forms the southern edge while the B3223 is the eastern boundary up to Foreland Point. The A39 lies to the north of this area.

2. The North-east Moor. From Simonsbath the B3223 as far as

Exford and then the B3224 forms the southern boundary as far as the A396 which runs up the eastern side. Again in the north the A39 makes the northern limit.

3. The Southern Moor. This is one of the more contrived areas but it is the countryside that lies south of the B3358 to Simonsbath and then south of the B3223 as it goes west to White Cross and then south of the B3224 as it runs through Exford, again to the A396 which forms the eastern boundary.

4. The Brendons. East of the A396.

5. The North Coast. North of the A39.

6. The Quantocks.

Because public transport is limited on Exmoor I am assuming that most of you will be travelling by car. For this reason I have tried to make the walks circular where possible.

I have graded the walks firstly by length;

Long: 12kms or more.
Medium: 4kms to 12kms.
Short: under 4kms.

Secondly, I have classed the walks hard, moderate and easy, depending on the difficulty of the terrain, the climbing involved and the map reading and navigation skills needed. With the last, however, it is wise to remember that what may be easy on a clear day will become tricky if the mists come down or if it is wet and windy.

I shall assume that you will be able to find your way to the starting point of the walks by car from the six figure map references that I shall give, but I must admit that the maze of small roads in parts of Exmoor can be confusing!

Left and right is in the correct direction of travel, but the *true* left and right banks of streams and rivers means as if you were looking downstream.

I shall not give the time that I think the walk will take, as each of you will need to work it out for yourself depending on the age and fitness of your party and whether you want to wander gently, exploring and looking at things as you go or put your head down and rush round as fast as you can go! I hope it will be the former!

Quite often you will be passing by places or objects to which I referred in the earlier introductory sections so you may need to check back to relevant pages but I shall hope to add more information wherever possible and indeed introduce new topics of interest.

With some of the walks it will be possible to shorten them by cutting off corners and leading back onto the route at another place. Even if I have not indicated this in the description of the route, by studying the map you will be able to make your own cuts, I am sure, if you wish. Equally so you might well find that you can cut into a walk from a starting place of your own choice, different to the one that I have suggested. Also it is quite possible to link into one walk from another and even end up at the starting place of that walk, if you can get someone to drive the car round. What I am really saying is that I hope that you will use this guide as a basis for walks that you can work out for yourselves, rather than following slavishly the exact routes that I have described. Obviously though I hope that you will follow some of my walks as they are all ones that I have enjoyed over the years or have found while writing this book.

Those who cannot walk or may not want to walk, will also be able to use this guide so that, with the aid of a map and what I have written here, you will be able to come on some of the walks with me in your imagination and find out more about this beautiful and fascinating place, Exmoor.

All that remains now is for me to wish you safe, enjoyable and interesting walking.

PART ONE:

The North-West Moor

> 1. **Chains Barrow. Pinkworthy Pond. Wood Barrow. Sloley Stone. Mole's Chamber. The Harepath.**
> **Length:** Medium - 5¾ miles/9kms
> **Difficulty:** Moderate
> **Maps:** Pathfinder SS64/74, SS63/73; Landranger 180.

START. There are two possible car parks on the north side of the B3358 between Simonsbath and Challacombe, where the road has been widened. The nearest to the start is at Map Ref 728402 just west of the entrance to Driver Farm, the other is nearer the drive to Pinkery Farm. This road, by the way, was one of the tracks that John Knight improved when he took over the lands of the Forest of Exmoor. It was, and still is for that matter, an important highway across the moor from the ports of Barnstaple and Bideford.

There is a post office and an inn at Challacombe while you will find the hotel - once James Boevey's and John Knight's old home - at Simonsbath, both within a few miles of the start.

It is only right and proper that the first walk should take you up onto some of the highest and wildest parts of Exmoor!

Start by walking back a short way along the road towards the east and going through the gate into the fields on your left. Climb gently along the edge of two fields leaving the hedge on your right until you come to a gate with a yellow waymark that will lead you into a huge field of over 100 acres with clumps of reeds in it. There are usually sheep and cattle in this field, even a bull when I last walked here! A few marker posts lead up to the boundary wall beyond which lies the open moorland. Unfortunately the cattle scratch themselves on these posts and they are often lying on the ground! I suppose at one time this field would have been open moorland but it is typical of the land which has been enclosed, reclaimed and

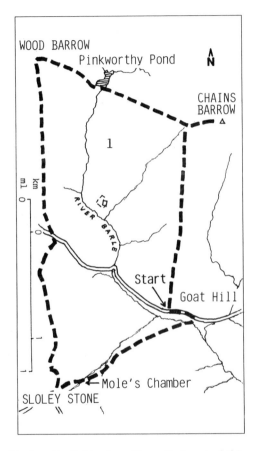

improved before the tightening of laws that control this.

There is a gate in the wall with a four-armed signpost. It is worth going through the gate and aiming slightly east and following the track up to Chains Barrow itself. You will soon see the concrete triangulation point on top of the Barrow at a height of 1,598 feet or 487 metres with a wire fence round it to keep the ponies and cattle out.

This is one of the really good viewpoints on Exmoor. You can look east towards Dunkery Beacon, south to Five Barrows and beyond to Dartmoor. To the west there are the rolling hills of Devon and with luck, on a really clear day, Bodmin Moor can just be seen.

Chains Barrow itself, the great grassy hump, is a Bronze Age burial mound. It is amazing how these early people built these mounds on the highest points. What hard work it must have been and I wonder how many weeks it took the tribes to build them? They must have been the final resting places of their chiefs' as near to the open sky as they could get.

Walk back down to the gate with the signs. It is unwise to try to go directly north west from the Barrow to Pinkworthy Pond. The Chains have the reputation of being one of the roughest, most difficult walking areas of Exmoor as well as being the wettest! The rainfall here can be as much as 80 inches in the year and with the iron pan just under the surface the water lies on the top of the peat and between the tussocks and all this makes for very awkward going. A lot of the area is covered with deer sedge and indeed is the largest area of this plant in southern England.

So back to the gate and follow the wall along towards the north-west. You can walk on either side but probably the south side is the easiest track.

You will soon come to Pinkworthy Pond which is also the source of the Barle. The Chains are in fact the watershed of this area for just a few hundred yards away to the north all the streams and rivers flow towards the Bristol Channel - the Barbrook, the West Lyn River, Hoaroak Water - but here the Barle and, at the far eastern end of the Chains, the Exe, all flow south.

As I mentioned in the introduction about the Knight family, John Knight arranged that 200 Irishmen should dam the headwaters of the Barle to form the triangular-shaped lake. Why he did this is still not clear. Some say it was to make an irrigation system for the farms below. Others put forward the theory that he was going to build a canal to carry iron ore for his ill-fated dabbling with the mining industry and this water would be used to feed the canal. Or that he would use water power to work some of the pumps, again in the mines. Who knows?

Ghosts are said to haunt the Pond. In 1889 a farmer drowned himself here and when his hat and coat were discovered on the bank they tried dragging the lake for the body to no avail. They then tried the extraordinary method of floating a candle stuck on a loaf of bread that was supposed to come to rest over the body. This didn't work! They then sent for divers who couldn't see what they were doing because of the clouds of sediment they stirred up. In the end they had to drain the pond and the body was discovered quite close to the side, in shallow water.

Pinkworthy Pond was drained again in 1913 when yet another person went missing and was thought to have committed suicide here also. Nothing was found.

In spite of these sad stories the sparkling lake set in a deep hollow is a calm and beautiful place and well worth a visit and a few moments spent just sitting by the water keeping an eye out for the wily old heron looking for frogs and eels.

There is a chance here to shorten the walk considerably if you wish and go back down the valley of the Barle on the true left bank, first on well-worn tracks across the moorland to cross marshy areas on logs and small bridges and over a stile into the fields that will lead you down to Pinkery Farm, now an outdoor education centre for Somerset County Council. You leave the centre on your left and go onto the made-up drive that leads you over a bridge and then back to the road. This walk is only four miles or 6.5kms.

However, I hope you will go on instead and climb up the badly eroded path to the west of the pond until you reach the wall and Woodbarrow gate that leads on to Wood Barrow, another Bronze Age burial chamber. You will notice a stunted beech here; all that remains of the windbreak planted by Frederic Knight.

There is a story told that Wood Barrow was rifled by a group of men from Challacombe who believed that there was treasure to be had there. Their leader, who was what was called a "conjurer" in the old days, which I presume means a sort of sooth-sayer, started to dig deeply into the heart of the mound from the top with the help of the men. As they dug they all began to feel faint. Suddenly there was a violent flash of lightning that struck right into the hole they were digging and a deafening clap of thunder. The astonished group saw that there was an empty ancient brass pot, green with age, lying at the bottom of their hole. The conjurer told them that it had been full of treasure but that, as the lightning struck and the thunder boomed around, the spirits who guard such ancient mounds stole it away. There is, in fact, a hollow in the top of the barrow so you can take this story as you will!

Turn south now and walk down with the thick bank and wall on your right side. Again, these were walls built by the Knights. Over Broad Meads and past a boundary stone until you can follow a track bearing slightly left down to the road.

Once again you can cut the walk short by walking back along the road past the drive to Pinkery Farm to your car.

But if you are feeling strong then I hope you will carry on over the road and go through the gate to follow the deep, rutted track south. Keep the hedge and the fence on your right as you climb the hill up to 1,432 feet (over 450 metres). There are fine views looking back at the Chains where you have come from.

When you come off the moor go through the right-hand gate and into a deep, rocky and often wet and muddy lane. This leads you down to the road near Mole's Chamber.

There's a story about this strange name for an area which has an evil reputation. One version tells how a certain Farmer Mole returning home late from market was sucked under into the treacherous bog that was supposed to be in the valley and disappeared. Here we go again. What about the pixies I hear you ask and were the pubs open!? Another version says that he was out hunting when he disappeared, while yet another puts forward the theory that he deliberately rode into the quaking bog to try to prove that it wasn't dangerous; silly man! Take which ever version you like, but you won't need to keep an eye out for the dangerous bog - you may get wet feet but I doubt you will get sucked under!

On the right you will notice a grey stone called the Sloley Stone. This was one of the forest boundary markers put up in 1742. It is quite difficult to read the carved writing but on one side it says "William Longe Oxenham Esquire Lord of the Manor of Highbray 1742", while on the other, "Christian Slowley Lady of the Manor of Gratton". It actually stood farther north at one time but was moved here.

There are quite a few rubble remains of old buildings around. One of these was the ruins of the inn called the Acland Arms which was built for the miners who worked at Cornham Ford mines in the time of Frederic Knight.

Diversion: The metalled road that goes south-west from here runs in a deep cutting and you cannot see that up to your right, on the north side, there is a remarkable hill fort called Shoulsbury Castle standing at the end of a ridge at 1,500 feet (472 metres).

Dunster

Selworthy Church

Porlock Weir

The Anstey Stone

The castle occupies a bleak, lonely spot and is well worth a visit if you have time. Its origin is uncertain as it is not the usual shape of an Iron Age hill fort, being almost square with rounded corners. It has been suggested that the Romans were here and although they had no trouble with the tribes that already lived on Exmoor, they might have felt that this excellent defensive position was worth using, particularly if there was already an earthworks there. All they would have to do was adapt it to their own needs and shape.

As you might expect there are also legends of King Arthur and even King Alfred associated with Shoulsbury.

The views from here are again magnificent; down to Dartmoor and you can even see Lundy and of course closer still the coast with all the hogs-back hills above the cliffs such as the Great Hangman. The diversion to the castle and back is about 1¼ miles/2km.

Main walk continued: Go through the gate in the corner just back from the Sloley Stone and drop down north-west towards the corner where the path crosses the stream. It can be pretty wet here. Go through a gate and you will see that the track runs in a sunken cutting to the right of a bank and wall with trees along it.

This is the Harepath that I mentioned earlier on in this book. It is fascinating to walk along such an enormously important route that goes back to Saxon times; it is one of the most ancient trackways in Britain. It acted as a trade route but more importantly men and supplies could be moved from one area to another with extraordinary speed. Whole armies could be transported to troubled areas running, as the Harepath did, from the Midlands, through Gloucester and Bristol, over the Quantocks to Exford and Simonsbath and then on to Barnstaple and Cornwall. One can almost hear the crunch of cart-wheels, the scrape of horses' hooves on the rocky ground and the shouts of the men as they "yomped" along this section that you will be walking.

It is easy to follow and you soon come down a steep coombe. Go through a gate, over a bridge and along the farm track that you will eventually reach and so on to the road. You should find your car a few yards along to the left where you parked it. (You could make a very short walk by starting off westwards along the road past the entrance to the Pinkery Centre and then turning left through the gate onto the track that leads down to Mole's Chamber and back along the Harepath to your car.)

> 2. Wood Barrow. Longstone Barrow. Long Stone. Chapman Barrows. Withycombe. Barton Town. Challacombe. South Regis Common.
> **Length:** Long (just) - 8 miles, almost 13km.
> **Difficulty:** Hard.
> **Maps:** Pathfinder 64/74. Landranger 180.

START. There is a car park that uses the disused bend of the old road on the north side of the B3358 at Breakneck Hole, Map Ref. 716411. What a splendidly evocative name. If you drive here from Simonsbath, just as you go over the well-marked boundary between Devon and Somerset, keep an eye out for the Edgerley Stone set in the hedge and bank on the north side of the road. This is one of the many old stones, like the Sloley Stone on the last walk, that mark the boundary of the Forest of Exmoor.

As with the previous walk you will find a pub that serves good food and a post office and shop at Challacombe. There is also the James Boevey cafe and Simonsbath Hotel back to the east just under four miles or six kilometres away.

This is another walk that takes you up onto high, open moorland but again with plenty of walls and signs to help you find the way.

From the car park walk back east along the road to the gate on the left. (You would have come down to this on the first walk before the cross over the road to go to Mole's Chamber.) Turn north through this gate and on the track for a while and then along the wall and the beeches across Broad Mead to Woodbarrow Gate and Wood Barrow. If you have not read about the first walk, have a look back to see what scurrilous behaviour went on here at one time!

Turn west now past the barrow and aim, across the rough pasture, at the gate in the wall, beyond which you will see the large mound of Longstone Barrow. All this area is at a height of 480 metres or 1,500 feet.

As with all the barrows on the Chains, Longstone Barrow was also a Bronze Age burial chamber built on the highest ground as near to the sky as possible to bury the chief. It is probably one of the largest on Exmoor.

From the barrow there is an obvious track that runs almost north

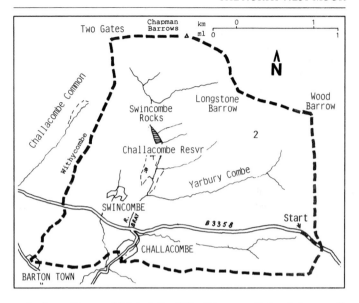

to the Long Stone, which is quite difficult to see as it stands in a small depression in an area of reeds and tussocks almost the same colour as the stone itself.

Long Stone is about nine foot high, and two and a half feet broad, but nowhere more than six inches thick. It is made of slate. This is the most impressive menhir on Exmoor though, to be honest, I do not find it outstanding. Its position might seem something of a mystery for, at first sight, one can see no real reason why the Bronze Age people - for indeed it was they who fashioned it - should have placed it here. But if, at some late date you have time to wander down the very steep-sided valley of the Swincombe, above the Challacombe Reservoir, then I am sure you will notice the rocks where the slate for the Long Stone was cut. Turn and look back from there and you will see the tall, phallic stone standing erect and black on the skyline. If these early people lived down here in the shelter of the valley then the Long Stone must have acted as an inspiration to them standing as it does on the skyline, as well as being a marker to show them the way up onto the open moor and eventually on to the Longstone Barrow itself where their chief was buried. So perhaps its position is not so

51

haphazard as it may seem.

Follow the often wet and muddy track beyond the stone towards the line of Chapman Barrows, one of them with a triangulation column on it, at 480m.

If you care to count, there are eleven barrows in all and along here they form the parish boundary between Parracombe and Challacombe. They are the most concentrated group of barrows on Exmoor and these and all the other barrows on The Chains surely indicate that a great many Bronze Age people must have lived, worked and died in the area.

As with the Dartmoor burial mounds many of the barrows on Exmoor were vandalised to get stones for building walls and barns. Chapman Barrows are no exception and apparently a Thomas Antell started digging into one of them to get stones for the farmer for whom he worked. He broke into a stone chamber in the centre of the mound in which they found an urn. Like the men of Challacombe rifling Wood Barrow, the farmer and Thomas thought that they might be onto a fortune in gold. However the urn contained nothing but bones, which Thomas said were sheep. Without doubt they were human remains, as indeed were the bones that the Rev J.F.Chanter found in 1905 in another of the mounds.

It is fascinating to try to speculate how the minds of these ancient people must have worked as they toiled to raise these huge monuments to their dead. You might come to the conclusion that they sought the protection of their gods and life-giving power to the dead. The sun and freshwater springs, both significant here at Chapman Barrows, give a clue that this was true. The Long Stone stands almost on a spring-head and all around the barrows are other springs.

Now walk along the barrows westwards and just down the hill you will see another memorial. This is the Negus Stone. It is placed at a lovely, lonely place and each time that I come here I find it quite hard to hold back my tears.

The memorial with its granite seat was put here by Colonel R.E.Negus of Oare Manor who was at one time Master of the Quarme Harriers. During the warm and beautiful summer of 1932 his son Robin went to a school camp and on his return it was discovered that he had polio from which he died, just before his eighteenth birthday. The memorial has the words on it that quite simply state that Robin "loved this place". And well he might, for Exmoor climbs away behind and ahead to the west you look out over the combes and downs of Devon with their patchwork of fields and far away, louring dark on the horizon, lies Dartmoor. The Bristol Channel stretches away to the north and farther west gleams the estuary of the Taw and Torridge, Tarka the Otter country. This is a haunting, wonderful part of Exmoor.

Walk down now south-west from the memorial to the gate that usually has a large piece of corrugated iron on it and a deep puddle between the posts! Go through and there are the signs of a faint track running almost south to another gate in the wall about 400m away. Go through the gates and over the fields by the walls until you can see the large collection of buildings marking Withycombe farm nestling in its windbreak trees. You soon join the concrete drive from the farm, with grass growing in tufts up the middle. It's a long downhill stretch to the road.

At the end of the drive you can see a gate just slightly left of you on the other side of the road and the route goes through it and across the field to another gate. Here you follow the remains of an old track that cuts diagonally up and across the next field. You must follow this to the corner of that field, through gates and then along the hedge to a more obvious track that runs down the hill towards the church that lies below you.

When I was last here the end of this track was unfortunately blocked by a wire fence, even though it is a right of way. If it still is, then, contrary to my usual advice, you will have to climb over it. The actual track goes on through the farmyard but it is probably better if you now turn left through the gate and into the field just this side of the churchyard.

The church at Barton Town is not very interesting but quite charming to look at. However, when I peeped in recently I was quite astonished to see a remarkable collection of ferns growing inside the church around the west window at the bottom of the tower! How long they will remain there, depends, I presume, on the vicar, but I do hope that they stay, for they give a splendid impression of being inside the Fern House at Kew Gardens!

If you want to have a look to see if they are still there, then enter the churchyard by following down the wall and going in through the little iron gate tied up with binder twine by a very marshy area, marked indeed by "Spring" on the map.

To continue the walk come back out by the same little gate (please do not try to follow the lane that runs out beside the farm to the south of the church) and walk east across the field and through the gate at the far side. Go into another field and to the gate on the other side where you will then cross the track I mentioned earlier. Enter through a gate again into another series of fields. There is probably a faint line of the track that you will see to follow, still going east, of course.

There could well be sheep or cattle here so please go gently and if you have a dog with you, do keep it closely under control. I am sure that you will make sure that all the gates are securely shut. These fields are all private farming land which has this old right of way running across it.

As you near the woods ahead you will be in a field where the hedges and walls have been removed and only low banks are left. On the edge of the wood you will see a large gate slightly uphill. Ignore that and aim at the smaller gate lower down the hill that will lead you into the wood and onto a steeply descending track. This is a delightful section of the walk with tall beech tree trunks looking like the columns of a huge cathedral. After the open moor it is a lovely contrast to be in the calm of the wood.

At the bottom of the hill enter the water meadows by the River Bray through a small gate. There is a right of way that cuts across the meadows to the building that looks as if it was once the village school; perhaps this was the reason for the path. You can take this if you wish and then walk along the road to Challacombe by Rooksfoot Bridge but I prefer to keep along the edge of the wood, dodging through gates and over a side stream (wet underfoot here) until you reach a caravan and camp site by a small man-made lake.

At the end of this field you will come out on the road on the outskirts of Challacombe. If you have timed it right you could walk on up the road to the pub for a drink and a snack. But steeling yourself, with great strength of character, to finish the walk, then cross the road and go over the charming little hump-backed, pack-horse bridge. There is a sign here that tells you that this is the way to Mole's Chamber.

The track climbs very steeply up in a deep, damp, wooded gully until you come out into a farmyard. Again please follow the signs and shut the gates. Turn east and follow the track as it climbs gradually up to South Regis Common by the sheep dip. You will reach a height of 430 metres with huge views looking back to Longstone Barrow on the other side of the valley to the north. No chance of losing your way here with the signs, track and walls to guide you.

It is a long stretch of nearly two kilometres from Challacombe and uphill most of the way! Anyway you will eventually reach the track that you might have followed on Walk 1 to Mole's Chamber and here you turn north (left) to coast down the rocky track back to the road, opposite the gate where you started. Turn left down the road back to your car - but not so fast that you break your neck by falling down a hole!

---

3. **Exe Head Bridge. Exe Head. Chains Barrow. Pinkworthy Pond. Wood Barrow. The Long Stone. Chapman Barrows. Two Gates or Parracombe Common.**
Length: Medium 5 miles/8km to Two Gates. 5½ miles/9km to Map Ref. 692443.
Difficulty: Moderate.
Maps: Pathfinder SS64/74; Landranger 180.

START. Exe Head Bridge on the B3223 north of Simonsbath. Map Ref. 765415. As you will see this is a walk where you will have to ask someone to drop you off and then pick you up at the end of the day. However, there is room to park a few cars on the verges and off the road on either side of the bridge, if you want to walk out and come back again to here. Simonsbath with the cafe and hotels is just down the road from the start.

This walk links together all the high ground of the two previous walks so as to traverse the spine, so to speak, of this part of Exmoor.

To start, go through the gate on the south side of the infant Exe, the true right bank in other words. This path is not a right of way but the owner has given the public permission to use it. It can be pretty muddy on the track for a while here. If you go up the hill a little you might find firmer ground to get round the bogs. The track bears up left away from the Exe and then follows along the fence to the source of the Exe (yellow paint waymarks on the fence posts). There are

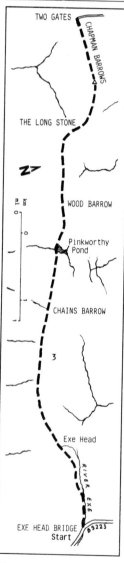

fine views over the Exe Plain here.

You will soon come down to an area of broad tracks with a gate on your right and two gates ahead of you. There is a signpost here telling you the various ways to go, with an M.W. on gateposts telling you that this is the Two Moors Way.

The head of the Exe is something of a disappointment. I think that one always visualizes clear water gushing out of the earth at the start of a major river. The Exe oozes out of the surrounding black, peaty soil in a large mass of reeds to your left! At least this is where the maps tell you Exe Head is, but there is a deep ditch on the north side of the fence that has more water in it, so I am not sure which really is the source.

The Two Moors Way runs north to the Hoar Oak Tree and south to Titchcombe, one of the areas reclaimed and enclosed by John Knight.

From Exe Head our walk is just a question of aiming west through the two gates ahead (red waymark paint) and then north west along the wall and fence to Chains Barrow.

From Chains Barrow westwards you can find all the details and information about the area in Walks 1 and 2. (Pages 44 and 50)

After the Negus memorial, go through the gate with the corrugated iron on it and follow the well-defined track north west to Two Gates. It is just possible to drive a car up to the gate but it is a very rough track. Probably it is better to continue northwards to the cross roads at spot height 368m. The road is made up from here and whoever is meeting you can drive easily to this point and park to wait for you. (You can also do this walk in reverse, starting here and being picked up at Exe Head Bridge.)

---

4. Brendon Two Gates. Farley Water. Hoar Oak Tree. Sheepfold. Exe Head. Blackpits Farm by Exe Head Bridge.
Length: Medium (just) 4¹/₂ miles/7km
Difficulty: Hard (just)
Maps: Pathfinder SS64/74; Landranger 180

START. Brendon Two Gates. Map Ref. 765433. There are broad verges to park on just south of the cattle grid and gates. You could, of course, do the walk in reverse and start at Exe Head Bridge Map Ref. 765415. As with Walk 3, Simonsbath is just down the road with the James Boevey Cafe and the Simonsbath Hotel.

The name Two Gates is found in several parts of Exmoor. Wherever there were gates in the boundary walls - and here you are not only on the boundary of the Forest of Exmoor but also Devon and Somerset - they were

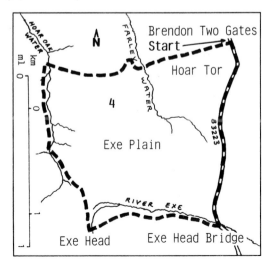

hung in an ingenious way. Two gates were fixed on opposite sides of the gate-post, both closing against another post. If the wind blew one gate open, it blew the other shut thus preventing any animals escaping and straying off their land.

This is one circular walk where it is impossible to avoid some road walking. You have to decide whether to walk along the road for 1½kms at the start of the walk or at the end. I feel that it is probably best at the end so that you get a feeling of exploration at the beginning, so that is the way the description goes.

Go to the north side of the cattle grid at Brendon Two Gates and turn westwards (left) to follow the stone wall. This is part of the old forest wall built by John Knight and, as I explained in the introduction to this walk, not only is it the forest boundary but also the county boundary between Devon and Somerset. You started in Somerset and are now walking in Devon!

You must now drop down steeply to the cleft of Farley Water Combe; a lovely valley. Cross the stream and start the pull up the other side bearing right and then back left to the wall again.

You will soon breast the top of the hill and start another steep descent down to Hoaroak Water. On the other side of the stream you can see what is marked as sheepfold on the map. This used to be a shepherd's cottage but now it is used for sheep. On a clear day you can just make out the concrete triangulation column on Chains Barrow about two kilometres away. If it is misty the wall to follow will be a comfort!

Just before the bottom of the valley you will find a hunting gate on your left, go through this to have a look at the Hoar Oak Tree standing within its wooden railings.

I hope you won't be too disappointed by this famous landmark! As I told you, oak trees do not grow well at this height on Exmoor! It seems to have reached a height of about 25 feet but it is rather put to shame by a line of huge and beautiful beeches just down to the north by the river.

This particular oak was planted in 1916 to replace the one that was put here in 1662. It continues the series of trees that have been here for centuries as an ancient boundary mark of the royal forest.

Go on down to Hoaroak Water and cross over to the other side and climb up steeply to join a broad track on the true left (west bank) of the stream inside the fence. You might have quite a problem getting across if the river is in spate; there are a few rocks upstream that might help you get over at low water. Do not go through the two gates that you will see to your right but keep left and follow the path to Long Chains Combe. On the way there, a gentle climb, you will pass yet another ruin standing like some ancient castle on a mound, again marked as sheepfold.

You are now on the Two Moors Way which runs from Dartmoor to Exmoor and I shall be including the Exmoor section of it in a later part of this Guide.

Cross over the stream coming out of Long Chains Combe which is marked as Hoaroak Water and also cross the stream running down from the south. This ford could also be tricky in flood.

The watershed is amazing here. Only a few hundred metres of bog right at the top of this valley separates this stream that flows eventually into the Bristol Channel at Lynmouth, from the Exe, which flows south to the English Channel at Exmouth.

This path steepens as you climb up the larger valley and away to your right you will see the gorge-like Chains Valley. This really is a most exciting area with the path climbing up along the side, with a steep drop down to the river below. It is the nearest feeling, on Exmoor, of being in the high mountains of Wales or the Lakes with sheer sides and rocky outcrops.

When you get up on to Exe Plain (a sign points the way to Exe Head) leave the broad track and aim right for the low bank that you can see and get on to the very badly eroded path that runs along it, to go south to the gate that takes you to Exe Head. Do not be tempted into following the Exe directly east as it is boggy ground.

It is quite a complicated area of tracks, gates and fences here and, indeed, it was probably a part of the Harepath and other tracks in Saxon times. Before the fence, aim left at the large gate with the signpost and turn left after it along the wire fence.

Yellow waymarks on the fence posts will show you the way. Do not go down to the River Exe, still just a stream, but follow the path right and skirt along above the Exe. Soon you will drop down nearer the water and after the hunting gate you come to a muddy area. And so to the road at Exe Head Bridge and with a brisk stride along the grassy verge of the wide road, built by the unemployed in the 1920s, you should soon cover the 1½kms back to your car.

PART TWO:

The North-East Moor

---

5. **Brendon Two Gates. Hoccombe Combe. Badgworthy Water. Lank Combe. Lankcombe Ford. Car Park Map Ref. 759452. Farley Water. Clannon Ball.**
Length: Long (just) 7½ miles/12km.
Difficulty: Moderate to hard.
Maps: Pathfinder SS64/74; Landranger 180.

START. There are two starting places; the choice is yours. You can either park on the wide verges south of Brendon Two Gates as you might have done for Walk 4, Map Ref. 765433, or there is a huge car park on the high ground Map Ref. 759452 so that you can cut into the middle of the walk as I shall describe it. Once again Simonsbath is the nearest village with facilities for food and drink. I cannot mention Simonsbath another time without telling you about the fate of the little dog that belonged to the Rev Will Thornton who was famous for his book *The Memoirs of a West Country Parson* and for being the first vicar of Exmoor. The dog "died of eating copper coins and drinking whisky"! What a way to go!

The first part of this walk could be difficult from a navigation point of view in mist or bad weather. The walk can also be cut short when you reach the road at the car park Map Ref. 759452.

Go through Brendon Two Gates to the north side and aim out right across the open moor north-east towards the stone column you can see some way ahead. When you reach it you will see that it is another memorial. *The wording tells you that it is for Colonel Robert Hillhouse Maclaren who died here on May 20 1941. Colonel Maclaren of the Royal Engineers had already shown great bravery for he had been awarded the Military Cross after being wounded during the First World War and an O.B.E. after serving in France before Dunkirk in the second war. During the early part of the war there was an experimental station for*

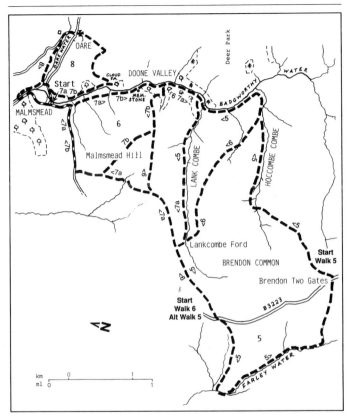

secret weapons at Lynton and Robert Maclaren was in command there. On May 20 he was in charge of a demonstration up here on Brendon Common being watched by senior officers of the services and members of the government. Something went terribly wrong and realising that the weapon was about to explode near the watchers Colonel Maclaren threw himself on it and was killed instantly, but saved the lives of all those around. His brother officers put up the memorial in honour of this astounding bravery and heroism.

There are many strange concrete foundations on Hoccombe Hill, probably the remains of the military activities up here in the war.

You need now to start swinging down northwards into the valley to the area of springs that feed the stream flowing down Hoccombe Combe. It is pretty boggy but hop across to the north side of the stream and you will see a gate through the wall ahead of you just up the hill north from the stream.

Go through this gate and find your way across the moorland aiming at the gap in the low wall ahead with its line of beeches along it. You will also see growing alongside the stream running down Hoccombe Combe another dense line of beech trees that probably started life as just a hedge.

This leads you down now into an amazing area of mounds and deep gullies almost like man-made earthworks or hill forts; they have been formed by erosion over the centuries. There were red deer here when I last walked down this valley, which had found a way across the stream and poured up Hoccombe Hill.

It is here that you join the track coming down from Badgworthy Lees and you are now in Doone Country! On your left you cannot miss the low walls and rubble of what was once a shepherd's cottage built in the 1860s, which became known as Lorna's Cot to satisfy the more commercial aspects of Lorna Doone! Further down the valley you will be amongst the overgrown mounds of the medieval village known as Badgworthy. *An excavation and survey in the 1930s showed that there had been fourteen little houses here and, of course, this is the number of cottages that the forty terrible Doones lived in, as described by Blackmore in the novel* Lorna Doone.

This remote settlement has an interesting history and mention is made of it at various times. One of the earliest records comes in the twelfth century when a certain Henry Pomerois gave a grant of the church at Brendon and the land of "the hermits of Baga Wordia" to the Brethren of the Hospital of St John of Jerusalem.

Hermits suggest a religious community and a document signed by Roberto, clerico de Bradeworda, means that there probably was a priest and later there is written evidence of a chapel here. Other records show something of further transactions when the land again was passed back from the Hospital of St John to a family called Bagworthy who at the time of Henry IV handed it on to one Robert Hartington, Lord of the Manor at Brendon.

Then what happened is not clear but, as with the medieval village near

Hound Tor on Dartmoor, the Black Death could have wiped out the population of this remote settlement, for from the fourteenth century onwards there is no more mention of the community and it just decayed back into the lonely moor.

There are tracks and signs galore at the end of the valley where the stream that comes down Hoccombe Combe meets Badgworthy Water. It is a very lovely corner tucked in the bottom of the valley with steep hills all round. The hundreds of Doone hunters who pour into Exmoor in search of the legend do not often get as far as this and many think that the northern end of the valley near Malmsmead is the true Doone Country whereas you now know it is really Hoccombe Combe!

To continue the walk turn north and follow the very obvious track along the true left bank of Bagworthy Water until you just come into the woods after nearly a kilometre.

The way now lies up Lank Combe and once over the footbridge take the path that runs left or north-west through the gnarled oak trees of Badgworthy Wood. It is here that you will find "The Waterslide" described by Blackmore as "a long, pale slide of water". It is not nearly so impressive as he makes out in *Lorna Doone* but all the same in flood the three smooth rock slabs, about 30 feet long ending in a final steep plunge, are exciting enough.

You soon emerge from the trees and the track follows the valley, sheer on either side. To your right you can see a series of rocks that look like man-made cairns on the flanks of Great Black Hill. Again I was lucky to find red deer peeping down on me from Badgworthy Lees when I last walked up here.

Keep to the bottom of the valley and do not be tempted to follow the more pronounced tracks to the north between Great Black Hill and Little Black Hill or steeply up Little Black Hill itself. Take the left fork on the small path through heather and bracken towards the wall and you will find a gate by the stream that leads you through into the upper parts of Lank Combe and on to Lankcombe Ford.

This was obviously an important crossing, for tracks radiate in all directions but you must take the small one that cuts up north-west and then swing down towards the south-west on the larger track that you will soon meet.

(You could cut the walk short here by continuing up the shallow valley of Lank Combe and then cut back to Brendon Two Gates by trying to find a way through the heather, eventually parallel to the road; awkward going.)

If you have climbed on up to the broad track above the ford and are following along that, you will pass a small cairn away to your left. You can see that it is marked by an iron post with a star. I read somewhere that this was put here to show where the ancient monument was, so that tanks on manoeuvres during the last war would not drive over it. Go on and you will see the road ahead of you. The car park I mentioned earlier is just north of here in a quarry.

You can again cut the walk short and return to Brendon Two Gates by slogging along the road or finding a way through the heather parallel to the road. However, I hope you will go on, for the next section is one of the few remote areas where you can get away from tracks, waymark signs and maybe even other people!

Cross the road and slightly south find the small green track through the heather skirting round the head of the steep coombe and then dropping down the broad ridge to the fords on Farley Water. It can be quite difficult to see in summer with all the bracken.

For the next part of the walk from the fords I leave it to you to find the best way up the valley towards the south. There are various alternatives but no definite track to follow, only paths made by sheep and cattle which can be confusing! If you walk along beside the clear stream where you may see trout and dippers, the true right (east) bank becomes quite steep and you will have to clamber along for a short section, but if you are fairly active there should be no problems. It might be better to stay higher up the hill where a sort of path contours along or you could even cross the Farley Water, if it is not in spate, and walk up along the left (west bank) to cross back later.

You will pass a huge mound, that looks man-made, called Alse Barrow. It is unlikely that Bronze Age men buried their dead here as they usually put their mounds on the high ground. This really is a delightful valley and there is a marvellous feeling of solitude. Pick your way across the side streams tumbling down the steep side valleys past Holcombe Burrows. Just below Clannon Ball you can see a grassy track running more or less east that leads you back with a gentle climb up to Brendon Two Gates.

---

6. **Car Park Map Ref. 759452. Malmsmead Hill. Yealscombe Water. Badgworthy Wood. Badgworthy Water. (The Doone Valley). Hoccombe Combe. Bradworthy Lees. Lankcombe Ford.**

Length: Medium 6¼ miles/10km
Difficulty: Moderate
Maps: Pathfinder SS64/74; Landranger 180

START. Car park Map Ref. 759452. Lynmouth is probably the nearest place for various facilities like shops, cafes, pubs and so on, though once again if all you want is a snack or a drink then Simonsbath is down the road; don't eat too many copper coins or have too much whisky, will you! (See the notes to the previous walk.)

You might have sensed my slight aversion to Lorna Doone and all that it has done for Exmoor! However there are some good walks to be had in Lorna Doone country and here is another one that links in with several others which I mention, so that you could start or end in many different places. Once again I have tried to come in by the back door, as it were, to avoid the crowds at the start of the Doone Valley.

Set off north-east on the broad track which you might have come along on the previous Walk 5, past the tumulus with the iron star mentioned before. There are several signs pointing out to you that this is Brendon Common and telling you the way to go for the Doone Valley; ignore this last sign and keep straight on along the broad track. There is a marvellous feeling of space up here with huge skies and "larks ascending." You might even see and hear red grouse.

You come to another dividing of the ways, after quite a long slog across the open moor, with a lot of black peat dust in dry weather. At the sign that tells you that ahead you would go to Malmshead and Brendon, turn right and onto the more obvious track running east over the flanks of Little Black Hill. Walk along parallel to Lank Combe and the wall.

Farther on you come closer to the stone wall and you should see a new gate with barbed wire on the top bar. Do not go through this

Deer Park Plantation

gate but continue left, downhill, on the track. The highest point of
Malmsmead Hill at 389 metres is away to your left now. Ahead the
valley drops very steeply down and there are tremendous views
looking away on the lower parts of the Doone Valley and even
Cloud Farm which you will be passing on another walk. The broad,
open fields above the farm could well have sheep in them looking
like maggots on the hill.

The track swings round the flank of the hill towards the south
and becomes very steep and covered in loose stones as it drops
down into the oak trees and then follows the stream of Yealscombe
Woods. It was cool and peaceful in the woods when I was here on
a scorching, hot July day with buzzards mewing above the trees.
The stream runs in a deep gully away to your right.

At the bottom you will meet the main tourist track that comes up
with its hordes from Malmshead. Turn right (south) to follow
Badgworthy Water.

Go through the gate and you will notice a barrier across the river
here to keep animals from straying upstream. You can see the area
of moor opposite known as Deer Park with its plantation tucked
into the corner where Lank Combe comes down to the main river.

You have now linked up with Walk 5 that went up to the right
into Lank Combe through the stunted oaks, so if you want to return
that way then have a look back at the information given there. In any

case you may want to have another glimpse at the Waterslide and again if you have not read Walk 5 you will find out all about it in the description on page 63.

But to go on. After Lank Combe there is a beautiful area through rhododendrons before the trees peter out. Later you will find a rocky, wet section of the path as it crosses Withycombe Ridge Water.

You soon reach the corner where Hoccombe Combe comes down to Badgworthy Water and once again I must ask you to look back to Walk 5 for all the details of the medieval village and the way that this area was connected with the Doones by Blackmore. By following the higher path round you will be back by the ruins of the shepherd's cottage on your right.

Climb on gently up and through the old gate in the line of beeches and cross the stream coming down from Withycombe Ridge and you are now on Badgworthy Lees.

The track is obvious as you continue to climb up to the wall and through the gate. Keep Lank Combe on your right and do not stray downhill too much. There are quite a number of paths and tracks here running through the bracken, full of flies on hot, thundery summer days, but you should have no problems in finding your way to Lankcombe Ford for the track is, sadly, a huge unsightly scar.

From the ford you can cut the corner off on a small path to join the wide track along which you started out. By turning left along this track you will be back at the car park in quarter of an hour or so.

7a. Malmsmead. Badgworthy Water. Memorial Stone. Lank Combe. Lankcombe Ford. Ford. Lower Ball Gate.
Length: Medium 5 miles/8km
Difficulty: Moderate
Map: Pathfinder SS64/74; Landranger 180

START. Malmsmead. Map Ref. 792478. There is a large car park with a picnic area and toilets just north of Lorna Doone Farm. This start will land you in the middle of the masses who come to follow up the Lorna Doone legend, though how many will have read the book I am not sure! It is probably best if you can come here well out of season as the extremely picturesque roads leading here are very narrow and winding; Exmoor is marvellous driving country, out of season. As you would expect, the tourist is well catered for here in this pretty little hamlet, with its ford and old bridge, from souvenirs to food and drink.

Set off south along the road. You can pay, if you wish, to walk along the river on private land; as you will see from the signs, it's up to you. If you decide not to, then on the bend of the road, turn in through the gate to follow the waymarked track over the ford and on into the main Badgworthy Water valley. Go through a gate and the path now runs in a gully. Soon you will come down to the river, by the new bridge constructed to replace the one washed away in 1952, whose remains you can still see upstream. Cloud Farm is on the other side tucked away in the steep valley below Oare Common; the next walk will take you there.

You will soon come to the memorial put up in 1969 a hundred years after the publication of Richard Blackmore's *Lorna Doone*. Sadly, as we have come to expect, it has been scrawled on by vandals; why do people do it?

On now past the end of Yealscombe Water and you will have linked up with the previous Walk 6 (page 65) that came down from Malsmead Hill and then farther on Walk 5, (page 60) so I shall have to ask you to check back to get all the information for this section.

Just before the little bridge you will see the footpath that turns up right through the gnarled oak wood past the Waterslide and into Lank Combe that you followed on Walk 5 (page 60).

Follow the valley up to Lankcombe Ford. From the ford go north on the broad path until you link up with the main track that runs north-east over the open moorland. It is quite a long slog on the deeply rutted track. As you approach Malmsmead Hill you can just make out a post on the top and you will come to a sign that tells you that ahead is the way down to the village of Malmsmead and also Brendon. The main track turns right but you must keep straight on over the low ridge and walk on down to the ford in a little valley. It is track all the way now to the road and the cattle grid and Lower Ball Gate. Walk back eastwards on the road down the hill on Post Lane to the corner where you turned into the Doone Valley and then return to your car at Malmsmead.

7b. **Malmsmead. Badgworthy Water. Memorial Stone. Malmsmead Hill. Lower Ball Gate.**
Distance: Medium 3¹/₂ miles/5¹/₂km
Difficulty: Moderate
Maps: Pathfinder SS64/74; Landranger 180

START. This walk starts the same way as Walk 7a, but instead of going up as far as Lank Combe you should take the path that cuts up earlier through the trees into Yealscombe Woods before walking up and over Malmsmead Hill.

The path into the woods is fairly easy to see. You will notice some small scree slopes on the other side of the river and about 100 metres ahead there is a fence with a gate in it and a barrier across the river. Obviously if you go as far as the fence you have gone too far!

The path climbs gently at first up through the oaks with the stream in a gully on your left. When you come out of the trees you find that the main track swings right and climbs up steeply on loose stones; this is the way you might have come down on Walk 6. If, however, you want a change then follow the little green track that goes straight up along the stream and then into bracken, and as you gain height, heather; terrible swarms of flies buzzed round me in a dense cloud as I came up here on a sweltering, sultry summer's day! Eventually you join the other track (that swung away to the right) and soon come to a new gate on your left with barbed wire on it. Here turn right and climb up Malmsmead Hill, following the rutted track in the heather. Go over the top to drop down the other side north-west until once again you will reach the road. Turn right, then back down Post Lane to Malmsmead.

8. **Malmsmead. Cloud Farm. Oare Church. Oaremead Farm. Glebe House.**
Distance: Medium 3 miles/5km
Difficulty: Easy
Maps: Pathfinder SS64/74, SS84/94; Landranger 180, 181

START. Malmsmead Map Ref. 792478, as for Walks 7a & b.

From the car park turn left and left again past the shops and walk over the bridge that crosses Badgworthy Water. You will soon see, on your right, the drive that leads up to Cloud Farm along which runs a public right of way. Take this road which crosses some fields and passes a small wood near the river.

Just before you reach the farm, after the gentle climb uphill passing over a cattle grid, take a sharp left turn with a sign that tells you that this is the way to Oare Church. The route now climbs again steeply up the side of the valley on a broad track towards the north-east just above the drive you came along. At the top of this track, which can be muddy, you will see the sheep pens and the track goes through them. There are huge views up here, at over 300m, of the surrounding countryside.

Go through gates now and walk down into the small steep valley head where the track makes a tight bend. It is here that you go left to follow a path along the other side of the gully by the trees. Go through a gate and a field keeping close to the hedge, then go through the gate that is away to your right, *not* the first one you come to. Follow the hedge down to the road and by turning left you come to Oare Church, which you will have seen ahead of you for some time already.

They say some 50,000 people a year come to visit this beautiful little church, for as you probably know, this is where Carver Doone shot Lorna as she was being married to Jan Ridd. This would have been an impossible thing to do if the church had been constructed as it is now, for a chancel has been added since Blackmore wrote the book and Carver Doone would not have been able to see Lorna from where he was supposed to have fired the shot. You will find a short explanation of all this in the church.

Oare is an ancient parish and the name comes directly from the Anglo-

Saxon word Are. Mention is made of the area in the Domesday Book and the delightful church has been here for some eight centuries. It is no wonder Blackmore wanted to use the church in his famous novel because his grandfather was the vicar here in the early 1800s and he must have known both the parish and its people well.

Walk past the church towards Malmsmead but immediately turn right over Oare Water by the road bridge. After about 100 yards, you will see a wooden gate on your left. You go through this gate and follow the path signposted Malmsmead, which crosses fields and runs through a plantation near the river. When you come to Oaremead Farm the path goes round to the right.

After the farm, where the track ahead climbs on up to County Gate on the A39, turn left and then back right beside the river again. You could, if you wished, cross the bridge and get back to Malmsmead more quickly by walking right when you get to the road.

Soon Badgworthy Water joins Oare Water which you have been following and the united rivers become the East Lyn that flows down to Watersmeet.

The path by this delightful stretch of river runs beside Parsonage Enclosure which brings me to a gruesome Exmoor tale!

There are various versions of the horrible story but as you probably have guessed, the Doones are involved: "Child, if they ask who killed thee, Say it was the Doones of Badgworthy."

It happened at Parsonage Farm, Oare. The Doones, on one of their terrible raids, rushed into the farmhouse to find it empty except for a child in a cot. Seizing the baby they stabbed it to death shouting out, "Prick the calf and the old cow'll mooee!" - hoping that the mother would emerge from her hiding place, which was, in fact, in the bread oven, and tell them where the household money and valuables were. But in spite of the death of the child, the mother stayed hidden.

To continue the walk (keeping an eye out for the Doones, of course!) walk along the river towards Glebe House, which means a dwelling built on the parson's land, and then turn left over the bridge to the road, left again and follow it south back to the car park at Malmsmead.

9. Alderman's Barrow. Black Barrow. Three Combes Foot. Kittuck. Tom's Hill. Larkbarrow.

Distance: Medium 5¼ miles/8½km
Difficulty: Hard, with difficult navigation on two sections in misty weather
Maps: Pathfinder SS84/94; Landranger 181

START. There are two parking places quite close to each other. The first is at Alderman's Barrow itself, Map Ref. 837424, or just down the road by the cattle-grid, Map Ref. 835422. Exford is the nearest village with a post office, shops, cafes, hotels and a youth hostel about 4½ miles or 7 kilometres away.

Exford is a pleasant little village where on the saint's day of the parish they used to hold a "revel" with many local attractions such as wrestling and fireworks. The Devon and Somerset Kennels are

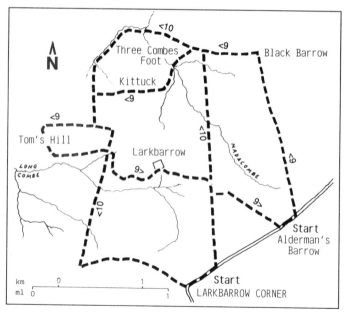

here and the whole area is excellent for hunting, riding, walking and fishing, and many tourists come here to stay or just spend a few hours in the village.

This is perhaps one of the hardest and most remote walks that are described in this guide, especially for two sections of it. It is one that I certainly enjoy for its challenge and variety. Part of the walk takes you along the old boundaries of the Forest of Exmoor.

Set off north through the gate by Alderman's Barrow, the Bronze Age burial mound from about 1000 B.C. and known as Osmundesburgh in 1219. If you start at the cattle grid instead, go through the gate there by the large Exmoor Park Authority information sign. In both cases turn right and walk along inside the wall until you see a granite memorial ahead of you. *It was put there in memory of Major Hilary Cox M.B.E. and his sister Avis Craven both described as "two happy people". Major Cox was Master of the Quarme Harriers in 1927 and their ashes were scattered on the moors here which they loved.*

You should just make out a faint track running off now northwards and although it peters out eventually, it will take you in the right direction to start with. You should also just see away to your left, near the start here, one of the small boundary or mearestones that are marked on the 1:25,000 maps. It is hardly worth walking over to it to have a look!

If you have a compass with you, (and for this walk I would advise you to bring it), you might like to try walking on a bearing along the boundary stones to Black Barrow. But on a clear day, follow the faint path I mentioned earlier which gets confused with cattle and sheep tracks when you reach the bracken. Keep north and you should cross the remains of the railway line that Frederic Knight started building to transport ore from his mines to Porlock. It was a failure as it proved too difficult and too expensive to lay the track and it was never completed.

The going is very awkward and bad walking for a while with tussocks and heather; not easy walking country where you can get into a steady stride. Be careful not to drop down too far to the west. To help you navigate visually you should see away ahead of you two small trees slightly to your left and another tree, dead ahead, growing by the wall. Aim at the single tree and that should take you directly to Black Barrow. As is so often the case you lose sight of the trees when you drop down into the slight dip about 300m out from the wall. You will soon reach the barrow, covered in heather and lying on the corner where the wall swings north. This has been quite an exhausting section of walking that would be tricky in mist.

Turn left (or west) and you can either go through the gate that you will see about 100m farther on, to walk along the wall on its north side or stay this side. There is no large track, I am glad to say, and the heather makes it a little difficult.

Diversion: There is not a right of way marked but it is a lovely walk to continue north instead, staying on the east of the steep-sided valley of Wier Water. Walk down to Robbers' Bridge or up to Oare Post; you will come to paths after about a kilometre.

Main walk continued: As you continue west you can see, on a fine day, away to the south-west an obvious clump of trees which are at Larkbarrow, where you will be in an hour or so.

A wall soon blocks your route if you stayed on the south side of the first wall and you turn right through the gate. You will have noticed on the walks that most of the Exmoor gates have two latches on them. One that shuts automatically so that if you just swing it closed it will lock itself and another latch that you must drop into its catch. I hope you will use both! If you look over left into the corner of the walls, by the hurdle, you can see the sign that points out the Larkbarrow Boundary Walk of six miles.

Walk west again, downhill slightly, to the lower gate on your left and you find a signpost that points out the way to Three Combes Foot. Turn in through the gate, south, and walk down the gentle slope to the floor of the valley. This is one of the most delightful corners of Exmoor with the steep sides of the hills all round and the three streams tinkling down under the little wooden foot bridges.

You will have seen, from way back on the hill, before you came down to Three Combes Foot, the clump of towering beech trees standing just up from the confluence of the streams. From here now you can see that they were planted in a circle round a wall about 25-30 metres in circumference. This is marked on the map as "sheepfold" but the Exmoor name is "sell" and this is one of the best examples to be found on the moor.

It was constructed and planted at the same time that Frederic Knight was arranging for the building of Tom's Hill and Larkbarrow farms. The trees acted as a windbreak and prevented snow from drifting and many thousands of sheep have been saved in the severe snow-storms that hit Exmoor by sheltering in this and the other "sells".

This is the sort of place where I love to linger and just wander about looking at the streams, the sell and the wildlife; there were ravens croaking in the trees when I was here, flapping off like black ghosts when I disturbed them. I hope you will leave enough time to linger, look and listen.

If you can drag yourself away, it's time to set off southwards, once over the footbridge and onto the steeply climbing, diagonal path past the sign that tells you that you can get to Larkbarrow this way. Towards the top, the path swings right towards the west again and leads you into the next really most difficult walking country on Kittuck. The word Kittuck comes from Kite Oak, another of those boundary trees mentioned from the time of James I.

The next kilometre will not be easy! The path peters out and you soon find yourself in an area of reeds and tussocks with deep gullies in between. In wet weather it is very damp going indeed. You are now aiming at the fence that you will eventually be able to see away on the far side of the open tussock moor. There is a gate through it and you may only just be able to make it out as it lies to the right of where the fence can be seen on the skyline. Do not be tempted to aim straight at the gate when you sight it, as this will lead you into an appalling area! Skirt round to the left (or south) keeping on the slightly higher ground and avoid the dense beds of reeds. Even so, it is bad going!

When you get to the gate go through and turn left. Walk south on a reasonable path; easier going at last! There is a great feeling of height here and you can see the line of trees where you started at Alderman's Barrow and almost the whole of the circuit you have done so far. Soon you come to the corner of the fence and once again you can see the signs marking the Larkbarrow Boundary Walk on the other side, by a stile.

Turn right and there is a gate on your left that you could go through and join the Boundary Walk if you wished, and indeed cut this walk short and go down to Larkbarrow.

However, to continue, turn west again and after nearly half a kilometre you will come to a gate on your left. You must go through this and follow the well-defined path south as the hill steepens.

There are huge expanses of open moorland to your right stretching round the horizon.

Ignore the first gate on your left with the stile and go on until you come to a large track or lane running east/west. By the gate, as always, there is a sign that tells you that Brendon is five miles, Malmsmead 3¹/₄ and the Doone Valley one mile. *This is a route that goes down to Badgworthy Water so it would be possible to link up with some of the earlier walks and come up to here and join the section from here onwards that you will now follow east. As long as you have someone who will drive round to pick you up. Or indeed you could go on down Badgworthy Water from here to follow to the ends of the previous walks; the possibilities are almost limitless!*

Go through the gate and walk east on the lane beside a very dense line of beech trees on your left that probably started life as just a hedge. There is a pleasant open valley to your right with one of the many streams flowing in it that unite to form Badgworthy Water. Soon you will come to Tom's Hill, the sad ruins of what was once a farm built by Frederic Knight. *Huge piles of rubble show where there were barns and shippons and the actual house itself. Great, grey beams lie on the piles of stones that must have supported the sturdy roof and all around are the beech windbreaks protecting the farm and the little paddock to the west. What a place to have lived and worked. It's always sad to see such ruins and sense something of the hard lives people must have led working against the harsh taskmaster of Exmoor. In the late 1840s two tenants tried to make a go of it here but found it intolerable and by the 1850s it was almost impossible to let.*

Both this and Larkbarrow Farm, which you will pass in a while, were still standing and lived in until the Second World War when the whole area was used for military manoeuvres including artillery and mortar practice. The inhabitants had to leave and the farms were reduced to rubble by both the shells and later the wind and rain. What a sad end to Frederic Knight's vision and dream of taming Exmoor and providing a way of life and a living for his tenants.

Now follow the track and soon it bears around to the right just past another gate with yet another sign-post with four directions on it. There is a stile on the left by the gate which is the direction you would go for the Larkbarrow Boundary Walk. Here you move away from the beech hedges and there is a feeling of open moor except that there is a fence to your left all the way to the ruins of Larkbarrow, also almost surrounded with windbreak beeches, that suffered the same fate as Tom's Hill.

No chance of getting lost as the broad track goes on beyond Larkbarrow and once again onto open moor but with the fence on the right side now. Soon you will come to another gate and you must turn through this to walk south for a short while before going through another gate on the left. The green dots on the 1:25,000 maps showing the right of way are quite extraordinary here. They appear to cut right across the corner where there is no path, straight through a fence and a wall with no gate!

The signs tell you that the Larkbarrow Boundary Walk goes through here and that you are on the right path for Alderman's Barrow. The track across the open moorland, happily with no fences now, is badly eroded and easy to follow.

There are some tumuli to be seen just off the track to your left but they are not very large and covered with heather.

A final moorland section will bring you back to the gate near the cattle grid and the large national park information sign and your car, either here or up the road near Alderman's Barrow. This is a splendid walk with huge contrasts that can be really very hard going in those two sections at Black Hill and Kittuck, with the delightful valley at Three Combes Head and the ghosts of the ruined farms and a reminder of Frederic Knight's dreams.

---

10. **Larkbarrow Boundary Walk.**
Distance: Medium 6 miles/9³/₄km
Difficulty: Easy to Moderate
Maps: Pathfinder SS84/94; Landranger 181

START. Larkbarrow Corner. Map Ref. 824415. There is a large lay-by where you can leave your car. Exford is the nearest village with all the facilities you might need so please have a look at the start of Walk 8 for details.

This walk, as the name suggests, runs right round the boundary of the 880 acres of grazing land that is owned by the Exmoor

National Parks Authority. It is here that it is trying new systems of land use and management that will not only both protect and conserve the moor but also be an economic way of farming.

There really is not very much to say about the walk itself, except that it takes you round a series of walls and fences, through gates and over stiles with signposts all the way! Because it is a boundary walk it does not actually lead you to any places of specific interest but it is always possible, by using the map, to come off the route to have a closer look at Larkbarrow ruins, for example, or to drop down to Three Combes Foot with its impressive "sell". (See Walk 8)

Having rather belittled this walk from the point of view of route-finding, I should point out that it does take you on to high, open moor at Kittuck and other sections, with the most marvellous feeling of space, solitude and height, with wide, sweeping views and into the heart of some of the wildest parts of Exmoor.

---

11. **Dunkery Beacon. Rowbarrow. Stoke Pero Common. Dicky's Path. Aller Combe. Hollow Combe.**
Distance: Medium 5½ miles/9km
Difficulty: Moderate to hard with quite a lot of climbing.
Maps: Pathfinder SS84/94; Landranger 181

START. The road on Dunkery Hill near the track that runs up to the Beacon. Map Ref. 904420. There are various lay-bys and parking spaces on the highest point of the road at Spot Height 443 where you can park the car off the road. Wheddon Cross and Luccombe are the two nearest villages with pubs, shops and post offices, both about 3½ miles or 5kms away.

This is the first of two walks that will take you to the summit of Dunkery Beacon and the surrounding moorland. Because the track that runs slightly south of west is the least steep, it is probably the most popular route to the beacon. At once you will be aware of the terrible problems that face the national park authority with such a popular excursion. Thousands use this track each year and it is now a broad eroded scar that runs through heather up to the cairn on the top at 1,705 feet or 519m - the only part of Exmoor, with Rowbarrow,

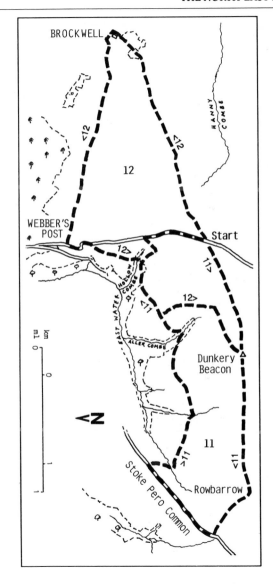

Dunkery Beacon

over 500m. There is not enough soil over the underlying rock to prevent the constant wear and tear.

Paths radiate in all directions from the summit and you could, if you wished, start this walk by using any of these other tracks.

The name Dunkery comes from the Celtic dun creagh *meaning rough, or uncultivated hill. Beacon obviously tells you that this was one of the fire signals that were used in the Middle Ages through to the time of the Armada and even up to the Napoleonic Wars, to give warning of invasion. In fact, in more peaceful times, they lit a fire here in 1977 to celebrate the silver jubilee of the Queen to link up with all the other beacons up and down the country.*

The views, on a clear day, are really breath-taking - they say that it is possible to look over 15 counties from here. The Malvern Hills to Bodmin Moor, Sidmouth Gap to the Black Mountains, Flat Holm and Steep Holm in the Bristol Channel - I could go on for ever it seems. There is a panoramic viewing table to help you identify points in the huge vista. What I love more than anything is the steep, dramatic drop to the north, down to East Water, where you will be walking in a while and Horner Wood beyond.

The memorial stone on the huge cairn was put there in September 1935 to commemorate the fact that Dunkery Beacon was handed over to the National Trust by Sir Thomas Acland, Colonel Wiggin and Allan Hughes Esq. The cairn itself is probably very old and in a map of 1687 Dunkery is shown with a tower on it. All around are the remains of other cairns and tumuli.

There were three mountain bikes up on the summit whose riders plunged off to the north down to East Water the last time I was on Dunkery. This is a new problem for the national parks all over Britain, though I doubt if their tyres erode the paths as much as horses' hooves and there are a vast number of trekking stables on and near Exmoor, but they do more damage than walking boots.

From the beacon go west on the track towards Rowbarrow and if it's a hot summer's day the air just above the heather will be shimmering with a heat haze and larks will be tiny spots in a blue sky trilling out their song. But come here in winter when it is bleak and cold with wreaths of mist over the stones and damp ground and you will be glad of that extra sweater that you put in your sack.

It is an easy route along the ridge and you will see two cairns showing you where the barrows are. You pass Little Rowbarrow on your right and then follow round to the right and this takes you on the left side of Great Rowbarrow, all Bronze Age burial chambers. The gentle slope and track north-west now leads you down to the road that runs between Exford and Cloutsham and you reach it just at the head of Lang Combe, a very steep gully. Turn right here and either walk down the road or try to follow the path that runs beside it; it can be quite awkward here in thick heather. (There is a quarry for parking so you could, of course, start your walk from this point if you wished.)

Diversion: *You are now quite close to Stoke Pero. This strange name comes from the Anglo-Saxon "stoc" meaning an area cleared of trees to which was added the name of the man who owned the area in 1280, a certain Gilbert Pero.*

The little church there was built at over 1,000 feet, the highest and most isolated on Exmoor, and if you have time you might like to wander on down the hill on the road to Cloutsham Gate and then turn left to have a look at it. I am afraid that it will mean quite a stiff climb back up again to continue the walk and it's quite a long way to the church. (There is a chance to visit Stoke Pero church on a later walk in Horner Wood.)

It is a very isolated corner of Exmoor with the church set in a hollow so deep that the unusual tower can only just be seen above the edge. It appears that this was one of the earliest Christian sites in the area, but not much else is known except that one of the earliest priests worked here in 1242 and that it was mentioned in the Domesday Book.

The church was rebuilt in 1897 and some of the old, medieval stones and windows were used in the construction. The inner door is also obviously very old. A fine and beautiful barrel-beamed roof was added and apparently all the timber for this was carried up from Porlock by a donkey called Zulu whose efforts are recorded for posterity on a plaque in the church!

Main walk continued: Having come down the hill (or back up the hill if you have been to Stoke Pero), nearly opposite the small fir plantation on Stoke Ridge, you will see a sign on your right (or left) that tells you that this is the start of Dicky's Path. The name probably comes from the fact that a lot of this land was owned by the Acland family and Richard seems to have been a popular name with them. It was Sir Thomas Acland, you will remember, who gave Dunkery Beacon to the National Trust.

Follow Dicky's Path which more or less contours round the hill after dipping into the head of Bagley Combe. There are good views away to your left to the Bristol Channel. The track climbs in and out of Sweetworthy Combe. After the beech trees keep to the main track which then runs quite close to the settlement near Aller Combe; you might like to wander down to have a look.

The name Sweetworthy, as you might except, means good enclosed pasture that was probably reclaimed from rough moorland. This area was once part of the Domesday manor of Bagley which was possibly deserted at the time of the Black Death in 1349; you will remember the village at Badgworthy too.

The settlement might have been built by the Bronze Age people who had moved down into the edge of the woods or it could have been a defensive fort used by the Iron Age farmers. As this and other settlements were built in good positions it might also have been used by the Saxons. As you see not much exact detail is known but there's a lot of conjecture.

Don't take the path on your right which climbs back up to Dunkery Beacon, unless you want to cut the walk short and return that way to your car, but go down steeply into and then out of the deep, gully-like Aller Combe. Keep following the track, still Dicky's Path, across the open moor. Away to your left you will see Cloutsham Farm and the East Water Valley that runs down into Horner Water and the lovely Horner Woods.

There are two ways now that you can start the steep climb back to your car. Just before the path enters the woods and drops down into Hollow Combe, by a gnarled silver beech tree with an amazing trunk on your left, you will see stretching up the hill to your right an intermittent line of small stunted trees. It is quite a struggle over bracken, heather, whortleberry and reeds but if you can, find a way straight up to hit a higher path that runs parallel to Dicky's Path about 300m away. Hard going, but when you find the track turn left along it. About a hundred metres before the path makes a right-angled bend left, quite close to the road now, you will see a fairly indistinct path again climbing quite steeply through the heather to your right; follow that. If you can get to the bend there is an even more indistinct path that also goes off right, to run parallel to the road. If you can't stand tripping over the heather, there is no other way than to find the road, I am afraid, and follow that steeply up back to your car.

The second way to get back to your car is to drop down into Hollow Combe, yet another of these beautiful, steep, wooded valleys, with a small bridge and little streams crossing the path. When you emerge out of the trees on the other side, the path steepens and there are a great many gorse bushes in the heather on your right. As the path levels a little, keep an eye out for a small, indistinct path that cuts up diagonally right through the heather; it's quite difficult to find so watch out carefully for it. Climb gently on that path with a feeling that you are going the wrong way, north-east, until you can see that the heather is not so thick on your right and cut back right, off the path now, to find the track I mentioned earlier that runs higher up and parallel to Dicky's Path. Turn right on it and follow along really quite close to the road and you will see a grey, weathered seat up to your left by the road. Walk on to the corner mentioned earlier where the path takes a right-angled bend and then either turn back sharp left and walk to the seat and the road and walk steeply back to your car that way, or try to find the first or second of the indistinct tracks that cut up left through the heather, either on the bend or a hundred metres along, which I mentioned earlier.

If you are feeling strong then you might like to branch off left from the road to have a look at the great stone heaps of Joaney How and Robin How; there is a good track running to them from Rex Stile Head. There are details of these cairns in the next walk. Not far now back to the car.

---

12. **Brockwell. Webber's Post. Hollow Combe. Dunkery Beacon.**
Distance: Medium 5½ miles/9¼km
Difficulty: Moderate to hard with a lot of climbing.
Maps: Pathfinder SS84/94; Landranger 181

START. The same as Walk 11. One of the lay-bys on the road at Map Ref. 904420, Dunkery Hill.

Luccombe which means "valley shut in by the hills", in other words Low Combe, is one of the nearest villages. It is well worth a visit because of the delightful cottages in Stony Street and the pretty little fifteenth century church of St Mary. Wheddon Cross is the other possible stopping place for shops or pubs. This is a name that was corrupted from Whaddene which was how it was spelt in the 1300s; it could mean "wet hill".

This is another walk that follows rights of way marked on the maps and also waymarked paths and will again take you to the top of Dunkery Beacon.

Set off just north of east on the path nearly opposite the popular route up to Dunkery Beacon, Walk 11. The area of moorland around here has many cairns and tumuli, the best known of which are Robin How and Joaney How just up to your left, great mounds of stones some 12 feet high and 40 feet across. *Both these cairns were known as Luccombe Barrows but by 1889 they appear on maps by these new names. Apparently how is the Norse name for a burial mound but why Norse words on Exmoor, I am not sure.*

The path, which is badly eroded, will lead you down a long descent with steep Hanny Combe away to your right and the pleasant village of Wootton Courtenay seen ahead of you. After a while you pass near birch trees and a quarry on your right. Keep on through the larch wood and by the deer fence. You are now down in the red sandstone area of Exmoor. You will reach the start of the drive to Ford Farm with a National Trust sign and a signpost.

Follow the sign that points out the path (north-west) to Webber's Post and walk on to cross the bridge where you turn left, again following the sign to Webber's Post. You climb up steeply and soon come out on the open moorland where you will skirt gently round below Joaney How and Robin How.

There are fine views from here looking north to the flat, alluvial plain of Porlock Vale, the white church of Selworthy with Selworthy Beacon towering above. Hollow Girt drops away to your right. (I see that the edition of the 1:25,000 map which I have misprints it as Hollow Grit. This is quite clearly wrong as "girt" is a marvellous west country corruption of "great".)

The path begins to climb and you will be looking down on Webber's Post where there is a large car park so you could start this walk from there, if you wished. However, at this stage do not go down to it but carry on to the road. *The name Webber's Post comes from Tom Webber who lived in Brompton Regis from 1812 to 1863 and who was a famous staghunter. It is a delightful area of pine and silver birch trees with many places for picnics. The Cloutsham nature trail starts from here and there are information boards with details and maps in the car park.*

Turn north when you reach the road and a few hundred metres round the bend that you come to, you will find the sign on your right pointing out Dicky's Path to Stoke Ridge which you take up Easter Hill. The sign is difficult to see because it is set well back in the bracken. Down below you is East Water which joins Horner Water. *There is a story of a person being thrown off his horse into the flooded East Water and his dead body being swept on down to Bossington before it could be recovered. You would never believe this tranquil, gentle stream could be a killer when you see it in summer drought.*

If you have already been on Walk 11 you will soon recognise where you are as you drop steeply down into Hollow Combe and climb up the other side. In the middle of the moorland between Hollow Combe and Aller Combe, opposite Cloutsham Farm, a track comes up from your right and crosses the one you are walking along. Turn left on this new path and start the long climb up to Dunkery Beacon skirting round the head of Aller Combe. It is quite a pull up, so keep turning round to admire the view to the north!

For details of the huge cairn on the summit of Dunkery, please look back to Walk 11 (page 81). Take the broad, badly eroded track down to the left that runs just north of east. It passes below Kit Barrows to your left. So many of these ancient stone burial mounds have been robbed of their stones to repair walls and roads. It is sad to think that the immense labours of Bronze Age man to raise some great memorial to his chiefs have been nearly destroyed by unthinking nineteenth and twentieth century man. Kit Barrows have not escaped. Downhill now all the way to your car.

13. **Chetsford Water. (Embercombe Water) Nutscale Water.**
Spot Height 372.
Distance (a): Short 2 miles/3.2km
Difficulty: Moderate
Maps: Pathfinder SS84/94; Landranger 181

START: The quarries on the steep hill just south of the bridge over Chetsford Water. Map Ref. 848419. There is room to park one or two cars on the grass closer to the bridge by the National Trust sign, but the quarries are better.

Exford is the nearest village for facilities. Porlock is only five miles away.

A mile or so north from the starting place is Lucott Cross which the malicious ghost of Mr Lucott is supposed to haunt and where the baying of the Yeth Hounds can be heard on dank nights when the

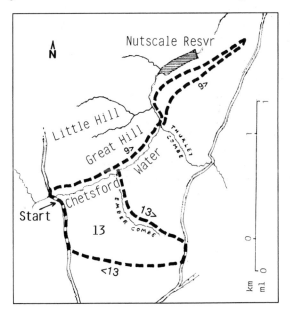

mists are swirling round.

There are three possibilities for walks here, all short so they are excellent for an evening stroll.

Cross over the bridge and turn right. There is a wet, muddy section but you will soon be over it and you see the path setting off beside the stream.

After a few hundred yards the valley narrows and steepens and you are into a marvellous, lonely, secret combe. This is one of the delights of Exmoor. The steep valleys, where the soft rocks have been eroded, give a splendid feeling of isolation and solitude. You can be only a few hundred yards from a road and yet feel utterly alone.

Chetsford Water, which means a stony or gravelly stream from the Anglo-Saxon word 'chesley' (Chesil Beach must come from that), tinkles along in quite a deep gully on the floor of a fairly wide, flat, alluvial plain as the valley broadens out. Every now and again there are deep pools where you could wallow in hot weather. The bottom of the valley has many hawthorn and rowan trees. It would be a splendid place to camp on the flat, green, grassy bank by the stream.

The path wanders on and crosses over Embercombe Water which flows down on your right; another delightful, steep valley. There are stepping stones across but it might be a problem getting over in heavy rain with the stream in flood.

Turn right now and follow the path up Embercombe Water. Just up to your left on the flanks of Honeycombe Hill there is a Bronze Age stone row unique to Exmoor. It lies SW/NE on a west facing slope and is more like the rows found on Dartmoor.

It is a slow and steady climb now up to Embercombe Head. At the top you will come to a surfaced road by a wide grassy lay-by. Turn right and walk along the road for about 100m keeping your eyes open for a track that runs off on either side of the road. The one on the left is deep and badly eroded, cutting a gully in the bank by the road. You must now turn right and set off across the wide open heather moor. This path will lead you round below Bendels Barrows and eventually to the road where, by turning right, you will soon drop back down to your car.

b) This is a walk where you will have to persuade someone to drive round to the other end to pick you up! They will have to wait at Spot

Height 372. Map Ref. 868435. This is on a lonely and not very frequented road and there are plenty of good places to pull off and sit for a while and look north across to Wales or away out to the west and the wild areas of Exmoor.

Distance (b): 2 miles/3.2km
Difficulty: Easy

Set off as for the previous walk and wander down Chetsford Water. Instead of turning up Embercombe Water carry on down the delightful, secret valley of Nutscale Water which is the name given to the stream after the two have united. Lower down the valley, hazels thrive and hence the name, again from the Anglo-Saxon, 'knutu', a nut. There are tracks on either side of the stream and the path criss-crosses in several places. You would probably be better off on the true left bank.

After a while you will come to a ford marked on the map where the stream from Thurley Combe (corruption of Thorn-ley; there are certainly plenty of hawthorns here) joins Nutscale Water and you will see climbing diagonally up the slope opposite you, on the other side, a broad and obvious track.

Decisions again! You can now climb on up the broad, stony track to emerge on the open moor and follow it for over half a mile until you come to a made-up road that runs west down to Nutscale Reservoir. Here you turn right and walk along to Spot Height 372 where, with luck, someone will be waiting for you. I hope they are because, as I said, it is quite a lonely, unfrequented road and a long way to walk back to civilization!

Diversion: While the views across the Bristol Channel to Wales are good when you are on the track, you do not see Nutscale Reservoir, built in 1941 to provide water for Minehead, nor the steep and lovely valley in which it lies. So after the ford mentioned above, when you reach the right-angled bend in the broad track, turn left downhill towards the bottom of the valley where you will see a gate after another ford and a broad, steep track climbing up the other side. About a hundred metres from the bottom of the valley there is a stony, double rutted track running steeply up to your right. Slightly farther left forking off that track you should be able to make out a small rather indistinct path climbing gently up through gorse bushes, rocks and heather. This path runs parallel to the top track mentioned earlier but it is far enough left for you to be able to look down on the reservoir and is better than walking on the stony track.

You will notice that the whole area of the reservoir is surrounded by great coils of barbed wire and you are not able to approach the water or walk along the banks. I suppose it is necessary, but it saddens me to see such a brutal fence looking like the trenches of World War One.

Follow the path once again until you come to the made-up road leading down to the reservoir or make your way back over the heather to the broad, stony track and then turn right to get back to Spot Height 372.

Distance (c): Short 1³/₄ miles/2.6km
Difficulty: Easy

There is nothing to add for this walk except to suggest that you might like to stroll gently down to the ford on Nutscale Water, near the reservoir and then retrace your steps back again. The views always look different when you are facing the other way and this is such a lovely, lonely valley I can think of no better way than spending an hour or two lingering here just taking in the beauty and solitude.

---

14. **Webber's Post. Horner Hill. Horner. Luccombe Plantation.**
Distance: Short. 2 miles/3¹/₄km
Difficulty: Easy
Maps: Pathfinder SS84/94; Landranger 181

START. The car park at Webber's Post. Map Ref. 903438. This is an extremely beautiful corner of Exmoor with its pine and silver birch trees. I always get a feeling of being in France or Spain when I am here on fine, warm, sunny days with the scent of hot pines heavy in the air. All this area is part of the National Trust Holnicote Estate and the woods and hills around here are laced with paths. You could wander at will and make up many different circuits. Many of

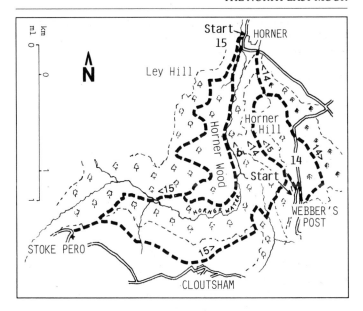

the paths have been named after members of the Acland family (you will remember Dicky's Path on Dunkery) or other incidents or memories for the family. Both on the 1:25,000 maps and the Waymarked Walks booklets you will see a maze of paths marked, most linking together so there will be nothing new in the two walks I shall suggest in this area. Horner, a very pleasant little hamlet, is close and indeed you could stop here on this walk to have a snack and a drink at the cafes there. The Green has been well preserved and makes a splendid focal point. It is a grand centre for fishing and riding. Luccombe, mentioned before, is also close to the start.

Before you start go over to the left to look down on Horner Water valley with its thickly packed oak trees that, in summer, look like a solid, green mantle cloaking the hills and valley floor. There is a small path to your right that climbs up through gorse to join the main track from this point which you can take, if you don't want to go back to the car park after looking at this huge panorama.

To start the walk go along the main track northwards and follow the crest of the ridge before the path goes down and you can see below you where East Water and Horner Water flow together. *You will pass the Acland seat sometimes known as Susan's Seat. It has written on it, "A lease for 500 years of 8,400 acres at Horner, North Hill and Winsford was granted in 1919 to the National Trust by Sir Thomas Acland, his brothers and nephew, to secure to the public the enjoyment of the beauty of these hills and moors and the preservation of their natural features".*

The views from Horner Hill are tremendous with the Horner Valley below, Cloutsham, Bossington, Selworthy and Porlock Bay. Ley Hill and Crawter Hill lie across on the other side clothed in heather.

You can hardly fail to notice, in several places, the open areas within the forest. These are firebreaks that have been deliberately cut to prevent fire from spreading if, for any terrible reason, one should start. I need hardly ask you to be extremely careful, as this fire risk is always a problem in dry periods.

Go down through pine trees to a sign that points you towards East Water to the left. Turn right here. At the bottom of the slope turn left down to Horner. If you don't want a cup of tea (I am afraid that there is no pub at Horner!) you can go on a little way and turn right on "His Honour's Path" - which is the way back from Horner.

Details of this hamlet are given in the introduction to this walk and of course you could always start from Horner as there is a good but small car park here with toilets, built by the National Trust and the national park authority in collaboration.

When you feel that your strength has been restored in the village go back up the path you used to reach Horner, ignoring the left-hand fork to Chapel Cross and find "His Honour's Path" or "The Judge's Path". This climbs on up through pines and silver birch until you reach the road. You can walk up the road to Webber's Post if you wish, but if you turn left and go down the road about 20m you will come to a track on your right with a wooden barrier across it. Take this and it leads you through the larch woods of Luccombe Plantation. Keep going right at any junctions and you will once again find yourself back at the car park where you started.

---

15. **Horner. Yeals Combe. Horner Wood. Stoke Wood. (Stoke Pero).**
(a) Prickslade. Cloutsham. Webber's Post. Horner Hill.
(b) Horner Water.
Distance: (a) Medium 5 miles/8km.
               (b) Medium 4 miles/6¹/₂km
Difficulty: a,b, Moderate
Maps: Pathfinder SS84/94; Landranger 181

START. Horner. Map Ref. 898455. There is a small car park here and cafes. It is a good centre for walking, riding and fishing. Porlock, Allerford and Luccombe are all equidistant for other facilities such as shops, pubs and post offices.

This and the preceding walk are both in one of the most marvellous wooded valleys on Exmoor. All the walks I have described so far have been on high, open moorland for much of the time, with descents into deep, secret, moorland valleys, but now we are off the open moor and into the wooded valleys that are such a feature of Exmoor. As with Walk 14 this is also in the National Trust's Holnicote Estate. The strange name Horner comes from the splendid Celtic word "hwrnwr" which means "snorer" and is said to be the noise that the river makes in spate!

Set off from the car park at Horner by turning left and walking for some 35m before swinging right over a pack-horse bridge across Horner Water. There are quite a few of these hump-backed bridges on Exmoor; most were built about 250 years ago. Turn right after the bridge, followed by a sharp left and you will start the fairly steep climb known as the "Cat's Scramble". *This is probably yet another link with the Acland family and the path could have been named after a lively little pony ridden by Lady Acland at the end of the last century known as The Cat.*

You climb on now through ash, oaks and beeches with a few holly bushes scattered about with views down to the meadows below and also the paths you will follow back on route (b) of this walk.

Here, and in other areas of woodland in Horner and Exmoor, you will see evidence of the old woodland management system called coppicing. Whenever I drive across France, I am always delighted to see the excellent, woodland skills that still can be seen there. Sadly in Britain some of these old skills have now gone and coppicing is not often seen in our few remaining deciduous woods. Every ten to 15 years depending on the growth rate and the demand, the trees are cut back to leave about half a metre, which will sprout and grow again. The timber can be used for fencing, pit props, firewood, charcoal and so on.

The path swings about round the head of a small side valley and you will be able to look across to Webber's Post. Pass over a wider path after an area where there are many tree roots underfoot. Soon you come to a bench where you can take a rest if you wish!

Always keep to the main path and soon after a contour round a further combe you come to another bench with again splendid views to Webber's Post and even up to the great stone mound of Joaney How.

When yet another path comes in from the right, swing left and go round the head of Yeals Combe. After here the oak trees are extremely bent and gnarled, weathered and stunted by the fierce winter winds.

You are now on "Granny's Ride" as you contour round and continue on over any cross tracks. Soon the path narrows and becomes steep as you drop down to Horner Water. You should go over the river by the footbridge.

There is a sign that points out the way to Stoke Pero and this is the path you follow uphill. It is marked on the 1:25,000 maps by the green right of way dots. Keep on ignoring the paths to the left. You will come to some fields and then a lane which leads you to the farm and the little church at Stoke Pero. (See page 82)

For the return route start back the way you came but instead of dropping back down to Horner Water (unless you wish to and want to link up with many other different ways back) fork right on the right of way across fields, around the head of Prickslade Combe and behind Cloutsham Farm. *The name means "farm by the kettle or cauldron" and comes once again from the Old English word "cietel" meaning a kettle. Obviously this refers to the raging East Water below the farm. It was built as a hunting lodge for the Acland family. Sadly on this walk you will only see the back of the imposing building which is now a farm. But you may have looked across the valley on the previous walks to Dunkery to see the interesting balconies and verandahs on the front of the house.*

After the fields you go right through a gate, left down the track and through another gate.

Before Cloutsham Ball keep to the higher right-hand path as you then drop down gently through some pine trees and past another bench.

The path takes a series of turns on Cloutsham Ball near the top (260m or 859 feet) where you bear left and drop downhill. You will soon see the nature trail sign. Bear right at this after the open ball and down through oaks again. The path crosses the river before climbing up steeply to join the main ridge track near Webber's Post that goes north up to Horner Hill and then back to Horner itself.

(b) If you do not want to go as far as Stoke Pero or have decided to shorten the walk then there are various ways that you can return to Horner; one on the left bank, the other on the right bank of Horner Water - and even variations with these.

After coming round the head of Yeals Combe the track swings right. Cross over the next path and you come to a broad forestry track cut out to give access for men and machinery and you must turn left onto this and descend. Obviously such a wide track is easy going and it will take you to where the other path, that follows Horner Water, joins it. Follow the river along until yet another path comes in from Cloutsham and soon East Water can be seen flowing to the confluence on your right.

Later on you could follow the signs to Horner Mill if you wished and cross over the bridge to do that along the old leat that brought the water to power the mill. If you carry on along the main river you will pass a camping area and after the gate turn right over the next bridge and you will soon be back near the cafe for a welcome cup of tea!

Variation: Another way to follow the left-hand bank of Horner Water back is for you to make a decision when you reach the footbridge that you dropped down to after "Granny's Ride". When you reach this bridge don't cross it but bear left and follow the river.

If you have been to Stoke Pero then you must come back to the bridge, cross it and turn right and follow the river down.

On both these variations you will link up with the description given earlier of the route back to Horner along the left bank.

Finally this last variation cuts out the steep climb back up to Webber's Post.

Having been to Stoke Pero and made the return via Cloutsham and Cloutsham Ball where you have some fine views down over the woods and back to Dunkery, take the right path after a seat. You drop steeply down between Horner Water and East Water and there is a confusion of paths but follow the nature trail signs down to the footbridge which you cross. Now instead of climbing up to Webber's Post, follow down on the right hand bank of the river and you will see a sign which says "Windsor Walk to Horner". Signs all the way now and some fine sections of path through pines which will soon get you back to the village.

In these beautiful wooded valleys, the whole area is laced with paths, nature trail and signs so that you could wander at will and work out a series of different walks. It is a good area to use when the weather is bad or too stormy to be on the high moor.

---

16. Dunster Park. Vinegar Hill, Bat's Castle. Gallax Hill.
Distance: Medium 4¹/₂ miles/7¹/₄km
Difficulty: Easy
Maps: Pathfinder SS84/94; Landranger 181

START. The car park near Gallox Bridge. Map Ref. 990433. Dunster is a busy tourist town in the summer months and parking can be a problem. It is quite difficult to find this small car park at the start of the walk. Come in to Dunster on the A396 from Timberscombe and keep an eye out for the lane that runs down beside the Foresters Arms and a telephone box on your right. The car park is on the left at the end.

Dunster is a lovely, small town full of history and some beautiful buildings, not to mention the fine castle. As you wander round, which I hope you will, there are many things to see including the yarn or buttermarket built in 1609. Dunster was an important centre for wool and farm produce at the eastern end of Exmoor and was once a busy port. The market was damaged in the Civil War. Then

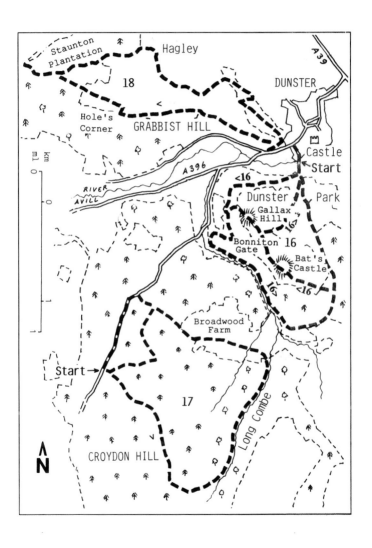

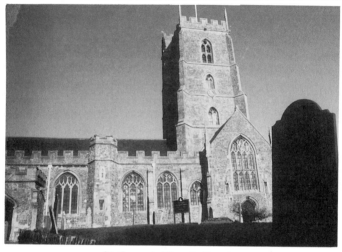

St. George's Church, Dunster

there is the Luttrell Arms built in the sixteenth century which was once the home of the Abbots of Cleeve. A restored water mill is also worth a visit. Above all, of course, there is Dunster Castle, which probably was built for the first time in 1070 on the site a Saxon hill fort. There is nothing left of its Norman origins; the remains are mainly sixteenth and seventeenth century. The Luttrell family bought the castle from the de Mohuns in 1376 and it remained in the family until 1976 when Colonel Luttrell gave it to the National Trust with the park. In fact the Luttrell family actually owned Dunster itself until 1950. The castle was besieged in the Civil War for six months in 1646 and was damaged and partly dismantled. A lot of rebuilding and restoration took place in the 1870s and it now still stands proudly over the little town which, in spite of fearful tourist pressure, remains charming.

Set off over Gallox Bridge which crosses the River Avill. *Both these names need explaining! Avill means "Valley of Apples" and was mentioned in the Domesday Book; a lovely name. Gallox or Gallax is more sinister and not lovely at all. It comes from gallows and is the name also given to the hill that you will be climbing in a moment where the owners of Dunster Castle* had their gallows.

The little bridge is yet another example of the pack-horse bridges found on Exmoor which you will already have seen. Pack-horses were the only way to transport goods and produce over the hilly country of the moor with very few good roads. Like sections of the Harepath, some pack-horse routes have become deep, sunken lanes by centuries of wear.

Keep on the track past a thatched cottage and across meadows until you reach the woods and the Park Gate. You will see a path with a sign pointing to Withycombe; ignore that and take the second right with signs that tell you that this route will take you to Timberscombe and Luxborough via Croydon Hill.

This is a wide, obvious track climbing gently up Vinegar Hill, a name that surely must mean poor, sour soil. This track is part of what was meant to be a coach road that was supposed to run from Dunster Castle to the Luxborough road started by George Luttrell in the last century; like so many brave projects, the money ran out and it was never completed. On the 1:25,000 maps the track and a lot of this walk is marked with the green right of way dots. It is a fine area of thick rhododendrons and remarkable range of trees including huge cedars. This is all part of the work of Henry Fownes Luttrell who created the deer park of some 348 acres in the 1750s. The idea was to farm deer here for the table though there had been deer herded to the north-east of Dunster in medieval times.

When the hill flattens a little ignore the gate on the left and go on through the woods.

Variation: You can shorten the walk and make variations if you wish. Where the track swings south, you can take the left fork and then climb up on the path after turning another sharp left. When you get to the gate and stile go right and out eventually onto open moorland and up to the prehistoric fort on Gallax Hill, this then leads you on along the ridge to Bat's Castle which you will visit if you follow the main walk. From here you can then follow down to the end of the main walk as detailed later.

Whether you take the variation or follow the main walk you should stand for a while at Black Ball, an area of heather and pines and take in the huge view, which is found a few metres off the track. From here you look across the valley of the River Avill and over to Grabbist Hill. Farther left Dunkery Beacon looms up.

Main Walk: Continue south and after some 400m by Bonniton Gate ignore the left-hand path and follow the main track down to the valley and the river below. This is a delightful section of the walk with King's Hedge Coppice steeply up to your left and the gently flowing stream to your right. It has been suggested that the name King's Hedge comes from the time of the Civil War.

When the track swings away from the river take the left-hand fork with blue and red markers. Farther on turn a sharp left on a hairpin bend onto a track by a bank of beeches, then almost at once turn right on a small path through some conifers and out onto the top of the hill.

By bearing slightly right you will meet the main path from Withycombe Hill Gate. You could, if you wished, turn right here and drop down to the junctions at Withycombe Hill Gate where you turn left by the stone wall with trees on it onto Horse Road. Red markers guide you past Horse Pond. If you do follow this way back to Dunster you will get fine views of the Bristol Channel with Steep Holme and Flat Holme and even across to Wales.

However, I hope you will turn left on the path to the summit of 210m and up to Bat's Castle where the views are even better.

Both this fortress and the one on Gallax Hill are probably Iron Age and are some 2,000 years old. It is built in an incredible, commanding position and seems to have escaped vandalism and damage for it is in an excellent state. It could have been used and even fortified at the time of the Civil War. No reason is given for the name except bats can be seen flying around it on summer nights! A walk along the outer bank gives you a fantastic series of views all round with the main mass of Exmoor to the south and west and across the Bristol Channel to Wales to the north and the Quantocks to the east.

Walk on north-west now on the path across the open hillside where you will drop down a little before wandering up to Gallax Hill fort a little lower than Bat's Castle at 174m. The views are as good from here and I suppose it was not a bad place to end one's life on the gallows! It has an eerie feeling and I am sure the ghosts walk here on moonless nights.

If you came up here directly from Vinegar Hill you can follow the rest of the walk down to Dunster now unless you would like to go on beyond Bat's Castle and return via Withycombe Hill Gate and Horse road as I mentioned earlier.

For the return from here go back to the col between the two forts and find the track that runs down through woodland lined with red markers to the north-east. It is a delightful valley and stream now all the way back to Gallox Bridge and if you have timed it correctly a well-deserved drink at the Forester's Arms or, more upstage, the Luttrell Arms Hotel!

Further walks in the Dunster area are possible. If you look at the maps of the countryside around the town, both the 1:50,000 and the 1:25,000 scales, you will see two large, forested hills where there are many rights of way.

---

17. Croydon Hill.
Distance: Medium 4 miles/6km
Difficulty: Easy
Maps: Pathfinder SS84/94; Landranger 181

South-west of Dunster is Croydon Hill and you could make a start from where the forest tracks meet the road at Map Ref. 969411. Follow the forest track south-east and then south until you come to the head of Long Combe. Turn north-east here into the steep valley and down past Withycombe Scruffets. (What a marvellous name! Withy means a willow of course.) After about a kilometre you will emerge from the forest where you go left across the fields to Broadwood Farm on the right of way shown. Beyond the farm, aiming north-west, you come back into the forest finally to meet the road. Turn left onto the road and walk back to the start, or you might like to find your way back on the forest tracks that branch off left before you reach the road. You will need your compass to make sure you are keeping more or less in the right direction; walking in thick forests can be confusing!

---

18. Grabbist Hill. Knowle Hill. Hole's Corner. Staunton Plantation etc.
Distance: Medium 4 miles/7km
Difficulty: Easy
Maps: Pathfinder SS84/94; Landranger 181

You could leave the car in the same car park at Gallox Bridge that you used for Walk 16 (Map Ref. 990433)

The strange name Grabbist, sometimes Grabhurst, may come from "graba" meaning a moat or trench and "hyrst" which means a wood. So possibly this could refer to the earthworks in the area meaning a fortified wood. It sounds a good explanation anyhow!

From the car park return onto the main A396 by the Forester's Arms. Turn left and walk towards the west until you come to the junction of the Timberscombe and Wooton Courtenay roads - about ¼ mile. Just before there you will see a broad, climbing track running off to the right into the woods. Take that track and then turn left onto the yellow waymarked path after a while. After that, the choice is yours to wander at will on the many paths and tracks to make a circular route. North of you is Hagley with the youth hostel and you can make a circuit to pass near it and once over the hill look down on Minehead and the muddy Bristol Channel not to mention the holiday camp. There is yet another Long Combe up here!

There are fine views back to Dunster Park and Croydon Hill and you will come across quite a few seats where you can rest and look about you!

You will find yellow, red and blue waymarks to help you find a route. The yellow ones go on to Selworthy, so for the return, once up on Hopcott Common, look out for the blue and then finally red to get you back past the plateau called the Giant's Chair and down to the road where you started. The distance is what you make it but just over four miles or 7kms if you more or less follow the circuit I have suggested.

PART THREE.

The South Moor

---

19. **Politmore Arms. Sherracombe Ford. Tumuli.**
Five Barrows.
Distance: Medium 5 miles/8km
Difficulty: Easy
Maps: Pathfinder SS63/73; Landranger 180

START. At or near Politmore Arms. Map Ref. 726356. There is room
to park off the road in this area at the end of Sherracombe Lane, but
be careful not to block it please.

Walk up the road from the pub north-north-east until you see the
entrance to Sherracombe Lane on your left; turn into it.

*The pub is named after a landowner called Sir Charles Bampfylde who
became Lord Politmore. You may remember that during the division of
Exmoor Forest resulting from the Inclosure Act it was Sir Charles
Bampfylde who with Sir Thomas Acland was awarded one of the large
"parcels" of land.*

The lane contours round to the small wood and leads you down
to Sherracombe Ford which you cross, by a bridge. (Sherracombe by
the way means a sheer or steep valley - and it is!). Follow the broad
track on the other side and take the right hand fork that climbs up
the hill, to the gate on the skyline. The right of way divides here and
you must go straight on and follow the fence north-west to the
corner of the field where you again turn through 90 degress after the
gate to go north-east, again along the field boundary fence. Across
two more fields, climbing gently and through gates. Please watch
out for stock if you have a dog and shut the gates. Just before the
road there are two tumuli on either side of the fence.

You go out onto the road and turn right. There is a great feeling
of height up here as you are right on the edge of the moor with huge
views out to the west and south with the main mass of Exmoor

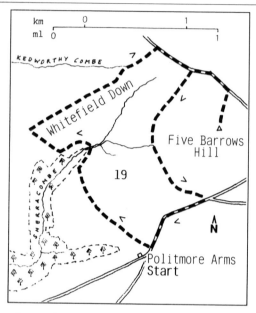

luring on the northern horizon.

Ignore the turning on your right for the moment (that is your return route for later on). Continue along the road until you see the way in that allows you to go and have a look at the Five Barrows standing at 493m (just missing the magic 500m mark).

You will have seen the Five Barrows standing out on top of the hill from many local viewpoints. Despite being called Five Barrows there are in fact eight, covering an area over 2,000 feet long and 500 feet wide. The name 'five' comes from the fact that from most places you can only see five at any one time. The area was also known as Span Head or even The Towers. They are, of course, Bronze Age burial mounds of about 1000 B.C.

When you have taken in the huge panorama and felt the magic of the place then go back to the road and retrace your steps to that turning to the left you passed earlier with the sign "unfit for motors". I am afraid that there is nothing for it now but to wander gently down this lane across Western Common to Five Barrows Cross. It is in a fine state of "benign decay", with grass up the

Two of the Five Barrows

middle! Turn right here and once more on the road to the Politmore Arms, which with luck might be open!

---

20. **Simonsbath. Winstitchen Farm. Picked Stones. Pickedstones Farm. Cow Castle. Wheal Eliza.**
Distance: Medium 6½ miles/10½km
Difficulty: Moderate
Maps: Pathfinder SS63/73, SS83/93; Landranger 180, 181

START. Simonsbath. Car park. Map Ref. 774393. The car park is on the north side of the B3223 just down from the little church on the hill. The church was built by the Knight family, to give a feeling of community during its efforts to develop Exmoor. The family are buried there. Just below the terraces of the car park is the village school also built by the Knights for the children of their workers and tenants. The name of the village comes from Sigismund, one of the heroes of early legends. Besides hotels there is also a pottery and craft shop and several places to have cream teas!

Set off past the school and the old post office back to the road and turn right toward the Exmoor Forest Hotel. Opposite a cottage there is a narrow gate by some ruins on your left that leads you into Birchcleave Wood.

The Barle valley below Simonsbath

There is a sign that tells you the way to go to Picked Stones and you climb up through mature beech trees planted, as you might have guessed, by the Knight family in the mid-nineteenth century. They are therefore probably about 150 years old and are growing at a height of over 1,200 feet, which is very high for beech trees to flourish as well as this.

There are red waymarks to follow now and there is one on a gate to your right, opposite a track. Go through this gate and into the field where you follow the hedge on your left. You go through the double gates and then bear right across another field to yet another gate. Red markers will lead you on to Winstitchen Farm.

On the other side of the valley of White Water, to the east, is Honeymead Farm, another farm built by the Knights, and above the farm the little river flows from Cloven Rocks bog (788395) which is where Carver Doone was supposed to have been sucked *down!* "*The black bog had him by the feet; the sucking of the ground drew on him, like the thirsty lips of death——the glare of his eyes was ghastly——while joint by joint, he sank from sight.*" You can't get away from the Doones, can you!

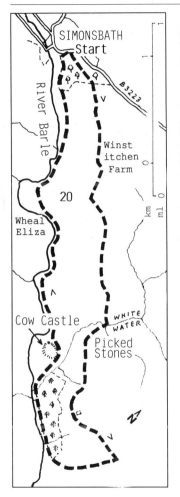

Looking the other way you will see Halscombe and Great Woolcombe rising steeply from the River Barle below you.

When you reach Winstitchen Farm you must turn right and follow the hedge through two more gates. After a while the hedge ends in a small fir plantation and starts to drop down to White Water, following a little wooded valley. You will find a bridge over the river.

Just up White Water from here there is an old disused quarry with a pleasant, grassy area and some old ruins. I love the way nature takes over in areas where man has made what were once deep, ugly scars in the countryside and turns them back into something beautiful. This is now a tranquil, gentle place.

You could cut the walk short here by following down White Water before you cross it down to the River Barle and then linking up with the last part of the walk described later.

However, if you go on, you turn right after the gate, having crossed the river and follow the track up to Pickedstones (Picketstones) Farm. You can see Cow Castle (where you will be walking in a while) by the River Barle to your right. *The farm was built in the mid-nineteenth century when there was quite a thriving mining industry in the area and the name, as you might have guessed, comes from the fact that there are many outcrops of rock in the area and that in some*

Cow Castle, the Iron Age fort on the Barle from the north

of the fields the stones were removed to try to improve the land.

At the farm you cross the yard and then set off along the lane. Following the red markers, go right through a gate, cross a field and finally through another gate onto the open moorland of Braddimore. There are fine views from here.

At a red post you must turn right and go downhill. The track ahead goes to Landacre Bridge, so once again you could shorten the walk if you have a friend who will pick you up there, but you would miss a most interesting section.

You can see below you, where the Barle and Sherdon Water flow together at Sherdon Hutch, a marvellous place for swimming - though because it is so popular it does get crowded.

The name Barle is corrupted from Barghel, as it was known in the thirteenth century; the stream from the moors. Sherdon also has an interesting derivation. The Anglo-Saxon word for a boundary is "scir" (we get shire from it) and Sherdon Water was one of the ancient boundaries of the Forest of Exmoor. Again in 1298 it was called Schureburn. Where the two rivers joined it was known as Schureburnesfet, now Sherdon hutch. Finally, Hutch is a local word for a sluicegate!

Soon you will meet the track that comes in from your left, also from Landacre Bridge, which you can see at various stages on the track; this is the Two Moors Way which I shall write about later. Turn right and follow the yellow markers up river past the large conifer plantation; it can be muddy here.

You will have to cross White Water, which, in spate, could be a problem, and you may have to cast around for an easy crossing place.

Pass by a small earthworks called, as you might expect with The Cow upstream, The Calf!

However, you soon come to its mother, Cow Castle. It comes from the Celtic word "caer" meaning a castle or fort (Caernarfon etc).

Cow Castle is a marvellous example of an Iron Age hill fort standing in a superb, commanding position on a steep bend of the Barle. It stretches for almost 1,000 feet and in some places the earthwork ramparts round the summit are ten feet high. In other areas you can see the dry stone walling that was used in its construction. When you stand on the summit you can appreciate why the Iron Age people built it here. The views are tremendous and therefore it would have been extremely difficult to attack successfully, though it has been suggested that it was more of a retreat into which the Iron Age farmers withdrew with their livestock, when strangers passed up the river or along the Harepath farther north.

(It is possible to reach Cow Castle by a short walk from Horsen Farm Map Ref. 785368. There are signposts to show you the way. Please park carefully there. You can then walk on to Simonsbath or return back to the farm. It makes a fine evening stroll.)

Follow the river now, by beech trees and banks. At Wheal Eliza the path keeps away from the river and climbs to a high level through some old workings. It is slightly awkward rocky going here as you reach another path. You are below Flexbarrow now.

Below, you will see the remains of the mine and the miners' cottages: all that is left now of the Knight family's ill-fated venture into the mining industry. They attempted to extract iron ore from what was once an old copper mine. Those of you who know Cornwall will recognise the Cornish word "wheal" meaning a mine. You might like to nose around the ruins.

One of Exmoor's more gruesome stories is set here. Living in a cottage just down river near White Water was a wretched man called Burgess who

View from Cow Castle

was a widower. He wished to marry again but discovered that the woman he loved loathed and detested his only child, a daughter from his first marriage. The only way out, as it seemed to him, was to kill his daughter, which he did and buried her body in a shallow grave. Unfortunately, the grave was discovered by two acquaintances who told him of their find. In horror and in a blind panic Burgess dug the body up and dropped it down the 250-foot shaft of Wheal Eliza and fled to Wales. The discovery of the grave with fragments of hair and clothing caused a massive search to be made and it is said that a weird blue light was seen flickering over the shaft and that led the police to find the body. Poor Burgess was hunted down in Wales, brought back and hanged at Taunton in 1858.

For a while now the path climbs up a rocky section to avoid the river bank which is too sheer to follow. Soon you can drop back steeply again to the river.

There are yellow paint marks to show the path by the beech hedge and various hunting gates to go through to reach Birchcleave Woods and back to the start, so finishing one of the classic Exmoor walks.

---

21. West Anstey Barrows. The Long Stone. Danes Brook. Hancock Memorial. Smallacombe Combe. Anstey's Gully. Ringcombe Plantation.
Distance: Medium 6 miles/9³/₄km
Difficulty: Moderate
Maps: Pathfinder SS82/92; Landranger 181

START. Junction of track and road just south-west of West Anstey Barrows. Map Ref. 855290. There are, however, many possible parking places along but off the road near here.

The delightful little moorland town of Dulverton is about five miles (8kms) away with many excellent shops, cafes and hotels. It is also the home of the Exmoor National Park headquarters, based in Exmoor House where there is an information bureau and a shop selling books, maps and souvenirs and where you can get your free copy of *The Exmoor Visitor*, a newspaper with a mass of useful, interesting and important information. Exmoor House stands beside the River Barle in lovely grounds and it is hard to believe that it was once a workhouse, built in 1855 for the poor and destitute of fourteen parishes around here. It remained a workhouse until 1939, then a maternity home and finally, before becoming the park authority's centre in 1974, it was the rural district offices.

In or near Dulverton is a fine centre to stay if you want to explore the moor and set off on daily excursions from here. The name, by the way, means a settlement near a ford on the bend of the river!

This is a walk in what one might call the southern ridge of Exmoor but it drops down first to the north and then to the south of the high open moorland.

Set off north up the track to have a look at West Anstey Barrow, one of the best in this area. You will see the white trig point off to your right. From the Bronze Age burial mound turn left or west and follow the track parallel to the road until you reach the very steep combe down which flows a tributary of the Dane's Brook in the deep valley to the north.

Keep an eye out for The Long Stone (yes, another and not to be confused with the one at the west end of Exmoor beyond the Chains.) It is quite

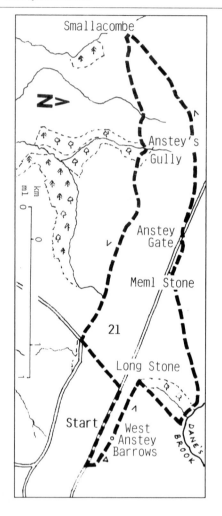

Landacre Bridge
Bossington Hill

difficult to spot from above as it is small. It stands above a spring in the combe that runs down to the north and this is probably why it was put here, for a north/south line was thought to be significant to these early people. Walk below it and it stands out against the skyline and becomes more impressive.

You have to find a way down steeply to the north now and there is no one definite track to describe though there are several that you might find to get you to the bottom. You will certainly see a mass of tracks running parallel to the main ridge, across the slope. They are probably caused by sheep and riders. There is also some pretty bad gully erosion here, where the heather and other vegetation has been worn away.

You will soon reach Dane's Brook, running in a delightful, deep valley full of silver birch and beeches. It is the haunt of dippers and kingfishers. Turn left here.

You reach a ford that you could use to reach Zeal Farm. At the ford turn left again to climb the hill up past hawthorns. The temptation is to follow the better track running beside the Long Stone Combe but you should resist this and keep going diagonally across the slope, gradually climbing almost due west. You should soon find the broad, badly eroded track even if you don't hit it at first. As a guide, you can see you are opposite a farm on the far, north side of the valley with a Dutch barn and also a wooded gully. As you reach more level ground the whole area is badly eroded by cars and four-wheel drive vehicles.

This scar will lead you up to the 13-ton granite boulder that acts not only as a memorial but a boundary stone for West Anstey Common.

Philip Froude Hancock was the fifth son of a Wiveliscombe brewer and banker, William Hancock. Philip Froude was quite clearly something of a character. He rode hard to hounds, played rugby for Somerset and England and was admired and loved by many people. He died in 1933 and in 1935 this great block of stone was brought here by a steam lorry that nearly blew up on the steep hills to reach this lonely spot. Of course, in the 1930s the roads were not as they are today! I wonder what archaeologists many years in the future will make of this alien granite boulder standing on this desolate moor?

Walk west again to Anstey Gate. The path to take to your left is clearly marked by the green and red right of way dots on the 1:25,000 and 1:50,000 maps. In reality you bear left on the slightly smaller track signposted Molland, opposite the drive to Lyshwell Farm. As you cross the moor you will just enter the head of Anstey Combe to your left as you dip down a little here. On now, dropping steadily across Gourt Mires but not into them I hope! Ignore any cross paths, but later on begin to veer left towards some fir trees on the other side of the valley where Smallacombe Combe meets Triss Combe. There are many tracks now but aim towards Smallacombe Farm leaving the steep combe on your right.

After the small quarry turn left towards West Anstey and aim at the boundary hedge which you more or less follow now as you walk east, climbing steadily. You will cross one small combe that runs down to Gourte Farm and then later the deeper gorge of Anstey Gully with its silver birch trees; another delightful spot where water runs away off Exmoor.

Just by the drive down to Brimblecombe the path becomes quite a wide track that vehicles can use. You now follow this along to Ringcombe Plantation then carry on until you reach the road that wanders south to places like Yeo Mill and West Anstey in a marvellous no-man's Land of remote, secret countryside on the edge of the moor.

Turn left here and follow the path north over moorland to another road where you turn right to find your car near West Anstey Barrow.

---

22. **Landacre Bridge. Withypool Common. Combe Gate. (Withypool Hill.) Waterhouse Farm. Withypool. Brightworthy Farm.**
Length: Medium 4³/₄ miles/7¹/₂km
Difficulty: Moderate
Maps: Pathfinder SS83/93; Landranger 181
START. The large, grassy car park near Landacre Bridge; pronounced "Lanaker", by the way. Map Ref. 816362.

Withycombe, where you will be walking, is the nearest village, and of course you could start the walk from there. But I thought that you might like to start and finish at Landacre Bridge because it is near the lovely pool at Sherdon Hutch that I mentioned on one of the earlier walks and if it is a hot day, a quick dip might be welcome.

Withypool, like Dulverton, is an excellent centre for those who want to stay on Exmoor and maybe go walking, riding or fishing. It is not so handy for the day tourists as coaches cannot park there and so it remains largely unspoilt.

The history of Withypool goes back to Domesday and earlier; it was called Widepolla then and was very much the capital of Exmoor until the seventeenth century when I suppose Simonsbath took over because James Boevey and the Knights lived there. The name, of course, means the pool by the willows! It was here that one of the pounds of Exmoor existed where the stray animals found on the moor were kept for a year and a day before they became the property of the warden, if not claimed. This little village is true Exmoor, surrounded by the moors and with one of the most beautiful of the moorland rivers running through it, the Barle. It is no wonder that R.D.Blackmore stayed here at the Royal Oak while he was writing *Lorna Doone*. There is a letter to prove it, hanging in the bar!

At the start the graceful Landacre (Longacre) bridge spans the Barle with its five arches built in medieval times. It was here that the courts called the Swainmotes were held twice a year to collect the payment for grazing and settle the laws and regulations for the royal forest. It seems to be something similar to the Tinners' Parliament that used to sit on Crockern

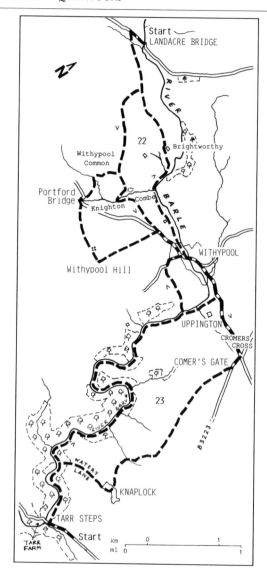

Tor on Dartmoor, but they met only occasionally while the Swainmotes
were twice a year. It was James Boevey who moved the Swainmotes to the
great hall in his house at Simonsbath.

Set off south-west along the road and then turn left on the path
signposted Withypool and climb gently uphill. After a while you
will come to a gate, through which you will eventually return, but
for now turn right and follow the signs again for Withypool and the
red markers.

Keep climbing up Withypool Common and there are plenty of
excuses to stop and get your breath back as the views down to the
bridge at the start and all the Barle valley are tremendous. *Just off to*
your right are the Brightworthy Barrows, yet more Bronze Age burial
mounds. In the thirteenth century it was called Briztenesworthy, named
after a man called Britsten. You might like to break away from the path
and wander quite steeply up to the trig point and the barrows at
428m (1,404 feet). There are usually quite a few Exmoor ponies to be
seen up here. (About a mile there and back.)

Diversion: You will soon come to the tarmac track that runs down
to Knighton Farm and there is a chance to extend the walk by about
a mile and a half here. You could follow this track to your right to
Portford Bridge and then strike up Withypool Hill to have a look at
the stone circle there, one of the few found on Exmoor. Cross the
road. After the bridge and the quarry on the right, a deeply rutted
path strikes up the hill. Follow this until you come to a cross paths.
Straight on goes to the summit of Withypool Hill so you must take
the broad grassy track to the right. On the brow of the hill look up
left and see if you can make out the stone circle. It is very difficult
to spot but if you now climb towards the top of Withypool Hill then
you should stumble on it. There are not many stones left in the circle
which is fifty feet in diameter and none of the stones is over two feet
high.

No one is quite sure what part these circles played in the lives of Bronze
Age people but quite clearly they were places of great potence and magic.
There are connections with the sun and moon but whether they were places
of worship or sacrifice nobody really knows. Legends and myths also grew
up around the stones; maidens turned to stone for dancing on the sabbath
along with the fiddlers who played for them and so on! As with the
Dartmoor circles I always have a strange prickling in the scalp when I visit

them and feel the presence of these early, ancient people who roamed and lived on the moors. After visiting the circle cross Withypool Hill and descend to the road near Waterhouse Farm to the north.

Main walk continued: If you don't take this extra diversion then carry on along the path to walk past a conifer plantation and then drop down steeply into Knighton Combe and up the other side on the stony track, through gorse. Red markers will lead you to the road which you follow to the outskirts of Withypool.

I hope you will have time to wander into the village itself to visit the interesting Church of St Andrews, maybe, and the Royal Oak, probably! You could start the walk from here but parking is difficult as the village lies in a steep valley though there is a small car park where you will turn in to walk back to Landacre Bridge by following the true right bank of the Barle for a lot of the way.

If you have been to the village, go back over the road bridge and you will see on your right the signs for the return route by the small car park.

There are markers and signs all the way now as you walk behind Waterhouse Farm. You can see Newland Wood on the other side of the river and here you will find an awkward boggy section beyond which you leave the river bank and walk across fields to Brightworthy Farm. There are red markers to lead you through the farmyard. Keep an eye out for the stream gushing out of the wall.

After the farm a sunken track will take you on your way but it can be muddy so it is possible to find a way in the fields to the left of the track; the views are better too.

Soon you reach the gate mentioned at the start of this walk and a gentle stroll back down to the river and Landacre Bridge.

A fine walk, this one. I like the feeling of the history of Exmoor one gets, from early times right up to the present with the barrows and stone circles, the Swainmotes courts, the Royal Oak with Blackmore's letter booking accommodation and the lovely Barle to guide you for a lot of the way.

> **23. Tarr Steps. Valley of the Barle. Withypool. Comer's Gate. Knaplock. Watery Lane.**
> **Distance:** Long. 7¹/₂ miles/12km
> **Difficulty:** Moderate
> **Maps:** Pathfinder SS83/93; Landranger 181

START. The car park on the hill on the north-east side of Tarr Steps. Map Ref. 872324. Dulverton or Withypool are the two nearest centres for all the amenities you might need such as shops, cafes, pubs and so on.

This is the first long walk in the book but if you have somebody who will drive round to fetch you then you could end at Withypool, which more or less cuts the walk in half.

It's a steep jolting walk down the road to Tarr Steps from the car park but if you have not been there before it is certainly worth walking right down to the bottom to have a look at one of Exmoor's most famous landmarks. (I wrote about the steps in the section of this book that dealt with the legends so I must ask you to look back at that.) The seventeen steps are most impressive and unusual, and is unlike most of the clapper bridges found on Dartmoor. The name probably comes from the Celtic "toher" meaning a causeway.

The width of the Barle here is over 120 feet and the actual bridge is about 180 feet if you include the approach stones. The slabs are about six or seven feet long and three to four feet wide and the largest must weigh over two tons. There is a lot of controversy about when it was built. Some maintain that it is prehistoric, others medieval. It stands at an important crossing of old routes and tracks. Often the River Barle covers the stones in flood and in 1947 quite a large section of the bridge was swept away when a tree trunk became wedged against it. Again in 1952, the year of the Lynmouth disaster, it was badly damaged. Each time it has been restored by Somerset County Council which has made a detailed survey of the position of each stone. When you realise the difficulties it had in making the repairs it makes one wonder all the more at the skills of early man who made the original Tarr Steps.

Back to the walk. Return up the hill, turn left just below Tarr Farm and cross the meadow to follow the permissive path that runs up the east, true left, bank of the river. At one time the path criss-crossed from one side of the river to the other at various stepping stones and fords but as most of them were difficult or impossible in time of spate, this path on the east side has been negotiated. This is also one of the sections of the Two Moors Way. There is not much to say about this beautiful wooded section of the Barle as you walk gently on through Liscombe Wood, Knaplock Wood, Great Wood, Lea Wood, Park Wood, Mill Wood, Pit Wood, Oakbeer Wood and by Ham Wood to Withypool. The charm and the magic of these lovely woods beside the cascading Barle running over shallows, foaming over rocks and sliding through deep dark pools, will speak for themselves. Yellow markers show you the way. Watch out for deer, dippers, possibly kingfishers, buzzards and ravens.

Out eventually onto the road and turn left if you want to get into Withypool for a rest and a snack in the Royal Oak or one of the cafes, or if you are going to finish the walk here.

If you are raring to go, then turn right along the road to Comer's Cross up a steep hill and then right again at the crossroads. Just after the cattle grid you will see a wide, stony track that forks off to the right which you take. After nearly a mile the track goes to the right but you must go straight on to the hedge which you now follow over the moor. Next go through the gate and go on down the track to Knaplock Farm. *I found a splendid snippet of information about Stephen Knapelock of this farm who was fined 40 pennies in 1335 for failing to attend a forest court! Jumping bail I suppose! I wonder what he had done?*

You now take the lane to the right of the farm called Watery Lane which will take you back down to the Barle and your earlier route. Here turn left and return to Tarr Steps. I hope the steep climb up the road to your car won't finish you off! I always find walking on a hard road more tiring than open countryside.

---

24. Staddon Hill. Larcombe Foot by Lower Kemps. Valley of the Exe. Lyncombe. North Higher Combe.
Distance: Medium 7 miles 10½ km
Difficulty: Moderate
Maps: Pathfinder SS83/93; Landranger 181

START. Rocks Bungalow. Map Ref. 872385. Please try to find a convenient parking place off the road as close as you can to the start. Exford, Withypool and Winsford are the nearest villages. I have written about the first two in the introductions to earlier walks but I must mention Winsford for it is one of the most beautiful of Exmoor villages. It is also a village of bridges for there are six - or is it nine - over the Exe and the Winn. The church is very lovely with many attractive and notable features; a Norman font, a staircase turret and a fine tower, a painted panel of James I and a Jacobean pulpit. Another Royal Oak is an excellent stopping place, while near Vicarage Bridge is a fine example of the many pack-horse bridges found on Exmoor. Ernest Bevin, who was Minister of Labour during the Second World War, was born in Winsford.

Set off south-east down Staddonhill Lane. Staddon Hill means a hill for bullocks from the Anglo-Saxon "stod". The tarmac road becomes grassy after Staddon Farm entrance but then drops down to run as a sunken lane with high banks on each side. It can be quite wet and muddy here. At the highest point of the hill there are fine views back north to Dunkery and also looking down on the Exe valley.

Diversions: Opposite the lane that runs down to Staddon Farm you might like to divert left and walk down the hill to have a look at Staddon Fort, an Iron Age settlement. (You can also cut the walk short here by going down to Staddon Farm on your right and joining the last part of the route by East and West Nethercote.)

The settlement is another of these impressive Iron Age earthworks built at 1,000 feet in a fine defensive position. The Harepath runs just north of the ramparts and this must be one of the reasons for its position. It was surveyed thoroughly in 1965 and this resulted in a few questions being raised, for there is quite a large gap in the defensive ramparts on the eastern

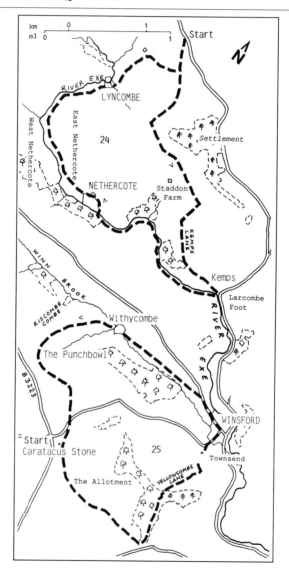

side. Suggestions were put forward that the earthworks were never completed. It still remains a mystery. It is sad that a thick spruce plantation makes access to the settlement difficult and also prevents the visitor from appreciating the full grandeur of the site.

Main walk continued: Climb back to the main track and go through the gate. After about 500 yards take the sharp right turn to descend first south and then south-east along Kemps Lane to the road at Larcombe Foot that runs down to Winsford.

Walk a few steps along the road and then turn right over the bridge onto the drive that runs along to East and West Nethercote Farms. It is a flat walk with the River Exe rushing away to your right. Keep an eye out for dippers, kingfishers and the wily, grey heron stealthily stalking fish and frogs with high-lifting feet. I wonder if otters are back in this delightful valley?

After about two miles you will come to the bridge over the Exe to the farms. Nethercote is Anglo-Saxon for a lower cottage.

Cross the bridge to the true left bank of the Exe and then turn left through the first gate to avoid going right through the farms. There should be red markers now. This route goes through three fields by the river and then crosses right to go through a gate to join the original right of way. Fork right and keep on the left bank - don't cross the ford.

This again is a beautiful stretch of the river with the steep Curr Cleeve away on the far side of the valley. There is a marvellous feeling of solitude and being away from people.

After a couple of fields you will come to Lyncombe Farm and you will see to your left one more superb example of a pack-horse bridge. On top of the hill on the other side of the Exe is another Iron Age earthworks called Road Castle, built on a spur on the bend of the river; what a position! The Harepath passed just below this fort as well as the one on Staddon Hill. Sadly there is no right of way over the bridge enabling you to go and have a look at Road Castle.

On through the farmyard at Lyncombe to follow the drive up to North Higher Combe. Turn right at the farm and the track running east will take you back to Staddonhill Road where you go back to the left and your car.

It is possible to start and end this walk at Exford for there are various rights of way that come from Court Farm down to Lyncombe.

> **25. Caratacus Stone. Yellowcombe. Winsford. Withycombe Farm. The Punchbowl. Winsford Hill.**
> **Distance:** Medium. 5 miles/8km
> **Difficulty:** Moderate
> **Maps:** Pathfinder SS83/93; Landranger 181

START. The Caratacus Stone. Map Ref. 889335. As this is a popular stopping place for many people, even if they are not walkers, there are plenty of places to park off the road. You will be visiting Winsford on this walk but otherwise Dulverton and Withypool are both about five miles from the start. Obviously too, you could start in Winsford, if you wished, but I thought that it would be better to have the village as a goal for a halfway stop for refreshment.

We start at another of the Exmoor mysteries and, as always, the experts have argued long over this one. The Caratacus Stone is difficult to date, but it has been suggested that it was put up and inscribed in the Dark Ages - in other words, probably in the fifth or sixth centuries. On the other hand the stone might have been put up long before the letters were carved on it. It is about five foot three inches long with one foot three inches underground. It leans at an angle towards the west and is out of plumb slightly south. It probably weighs about 800 pounds (363kgs). It was mentioned as a landmark on the perambulations of the thirteenth century. The carved letters were eventually deciphered as CARATACI NEPUS meaning Kinsmen of Caratacus. The N was missing for some time, having been broken off with a pick in 1890, but was found and restored to its correct place when the bit of stone was found in 1908.

As you might expect, legends have been associated with the stone, such as ghostly horses and carts seen at night near the place and, of course, buried treasure which probably accounts for the stone being vandalised and dug up in 1936. In 1937 it was put up again at the correct angle and the shelter you see today was built to protect it. Exactly why the Dumnonii of Exmoor carved the information in Latin that they were related to the famous and courageous Caratacus is not known, for the Romans had long since gone. Perhaps it was a warning to the Saxon invaders that they would be met with fierce resistance. Who knows?

There are two ways to start this walk. You can either set off east directly from the Caratacus Stone along what was once a beech hedge, over rough moorland, or you can go back north a little to join the path that runs across the Allotment for a mile. This a pleasant fairly flat area covered in heather that from August onwards is a mass of purple. Keep an eye out for the moorland birds such as the skylark and lapwing and with luck you may hear the evocative, bubbling call of the curlew.

If you decide to follow the laid beech hedge and bank, you might prefer to go through the gate you will find on your left after about 200 yards from the stone. It is more pleasant walking on the other side. Soon you come to fully grown trees on your right and grass underfoot. After a while you will see an iron gate on your right. You could go through this and then left through another gate into the field by two wooden gates; yellow marks show you the way. Don't take the broad track straight ahead, by the way. However, instead of passing through the iron gate it is easier to carry on until you will see the broad track over the Allotment coming in from your left. There are two small gates near here. Go straight through either one of them into the field and follow the edge until you come to a quarry with some rubbish in it on your right and you will see a small gate on your left, this is your track. Yellow marks guide you most of the way until here.

Go into the spruce plantation and drop steeply down Yellowcombe through the trees. This valley was known as Yarleycombe and it is the Anglo-Saxon derivation "eald" meaning old and suggests land that has been cultivated for many years.

You will just see Yellowcombe cottage to your left through the trees and when the plantation comes to an end leave the wider track and take the smaller path to the left steeply down to a gate. Go over the stream and through another gate which will lead you on to the sunken Yellowcombe Lane with high hedges on either side; it can be muddy here. Uphill now to breast the slope with a grand view down to Winsford. A rocky descent will lead you to the road at Townsend which you follow to Winsford past the Royal Oak.

In the town turn left and follow Ash Lane past the church. At the end of the town you will see a sign that tells you that this is the path to take to Winsford Hill via the Punchbowl! It has yellow markers. You cross several fields, over stiles and through gates and soon you will reach Withycombe Farm.

Follow the yellow marks round the farm and over the bridge where you will find a made-up road for a while. Turn right through a gate and a little later left through another gate. From now on it's a long climb up the rim of the Punchbowl, a most impressive steep valley. (You'll remember from the introduction how it was the Devil who was supposed to have dug out this deep valley to heap the rocks and earth up to make Dunkery!) You may be glad to pause on your way up to get your breath back and look down to Winsford and over to the Brendons.

Climb on and eventually you will emerge on Winsford Hill, right on the very edge of the Punchbowl. You can see Dunkery back to the north-west and the Exe Valley below. Various tracks join up here but you might enjoy branching off right to have a look at Wambarrows: three fine Bronze Age burial mounds.

If you have been to look at Wambarrows, return to the head of the Punchbowl and join the well-defined track that runs east. This soon joins another and as the track starts to drop down towards Halse Farm and Halse Lane turn right on a path that will take you towards Spire Cross on the main road, the Caratacus Stone and your car.

---

26. **Hawkridge. Dane's Brook. Castle Bridge. Brewer's Castle. Barle Valley. Marshclose Hill.**
Distance: Medium. 4 miles/6km
Difficulty: Easy
Maps: Pathfinder SS83/93, SS82/92; Landranger 181

START. Hawkridge. Map Ref. 861306. This is a surprisingly isolated community and well-named, standing as it does at about 1,000 feet on a bleak hill, with a few farms and houses, a post office/shop and a pleasant little church with a superb Norman door.

On the bend of the road after the church turn right down the broad track called Row Lane that runs along the ridge south-east. The lane runs right out onto the spur of Hawkridge Ridge and then begins to drop with tremendous views down to the Barle below, where you will be walking in a while.

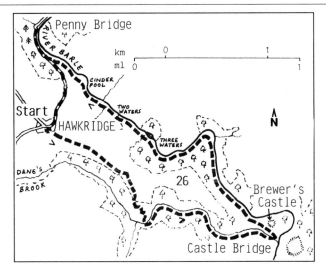

Just before some large trees there is a gate on your right signposted to East Anstey Common and with yellow waymarks. Take this path that will lead you down very steeply through woods to Dane's Brook. (Here it is possible to link up Walk 21 with this route.)

At the bottom the route to East Anstey Common goes off to the right to cross Dane's Brook by a bridge that apparently was built by the army in 1978. You, however, must turn left along the path beside the river to Castle Bridge. This is a delightful stretch of walking, as indeed most of the valley up the Barle will be. The brook here, by the way, is the boundary between Devon and Somerset.

You soon see Castle Bridge on your right and, if you wish, you can continue onto Dulverton that way by crossing over it. This makes a splendid descending walk down the Barle of about three miles. The confluence of Dane's Brook and the Barle is a wild and lovely place with thick trees all round and bare ridges above.

To return to Hawkridge take the sharp turn left with signs for Tarr Steps and Hawkridge. On your right, situated on a bend of the river, is Brewer's Castle and away downstream on the other side is Mounsey Castle. *These are yet more Iron Age earthworks from about 500 B.C. but they were named in more recent times after Norman overlords,*

EXMOOR & THE QUANTOCKS

Brewer and Monceaux. Sadly, both these remains are very overgrown with bracken and saplings and it is difficult to appreciate what incredible fortresses they must have been. There is a track to your right and that will take you to Brewer's Castle if you want to wander round and have a look.

Another interesting feature here is Thornton's Bridge which was built by the Devon and Somerset Staghounds to be used when the river is too high for horses and hounds to cross safely.

Follow the broad track now north-west but after 300 yards or so take the right fork downhill to follow the river and do not climb back up to Hawkridge Ridge unless you wish to return the same way you set out.

The path follows a huge bend of the Barle and then past some islands at Three Waters (where, indeed, the river divides into three), then Two Waters and on to Cinder Pool where you will come out of the woods into fields. The path leads away from the river to join the road that leads to Tarr Steps. Obviously you could go on to Tarr Steps if you wished, but if you want to get back to your car then turn left and follow the road up the steep Marchclose Hill to the village. It perches on the ridge with buzzards, if not hawks, wheeling round above it.

---

27. Round Oldberry Castle, Dulverton.
Length: Medium (just) 3 miles/4½km
Difficulty: Easy
Maps: Pathfinder SS82/92; Landranger 181

START. Dulverton car park near The Exmoor National Park Authority headquarters and information centre in Exmoor House. Map Ref. 913279. You may have read a little about Dulverton and Exmoor House in the introduction to Walk 20 but now here is a chance to visit this small town and wander round, for it is a pleasant centre with good shops and hotels and indeed could be called the "gateway to Exmoor." It is also worth calling in at the park's information centre.

Walking near The Punchbowl
Hurlstone Point

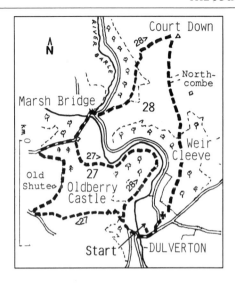

This is a short suggested circuit which would be grand for an evening stroll if you are staying nearby. From the car park come back onto the road and turn right and cross the bridge over the Barle. There are good views back to Exmoor House from here. Once over the bridge turn right again on the road that leads to the paths that run to Tarr Steps and Hawkridge. Just after the thatched cottage where the narrow road ends turn left up a steep lane. It can be pretty muddy here after rain and during the winter. *This is one of the old pack-horse routes from Anstey's Common to Dulverton. You will already have seen some of the little pack-horse bridges on previous walks and quite clearly there must have been a network of lanes and tracks crossing bridges linking the outlying farms and villages with the market towns such as Dulverton. The horses carried all manner of goods in panniers but I suppose wool was the most important commodity that was transported to the many water-powered woollen mills in Devon when the industry flourished in the seventeenth century.*

When you reach the top of the hill you will go through fields and eventually cross the drive leading to Old Berry Farm and then on again across more fields. Waymarks will lead you on by hedges and over a stile and from the road which you will reach eventually you turn right down the rough drive past Old Shute.

Follow along the edge of the plantation of conifers before which you will have had a pleasant view looking down on the Barle valley.

You then come to the road at Blacklake Wood where you turn right down to Kennel Farm. Here you make your return on the riverside path which unfortunately does not run really close to the Barle except in one place by a huge bend. Walk then along the edge of Burridge Wood until you join the narrow road where you started. Turn left over the bridge and back to your car.

---

28. Dulverton. Kennel Farm. Marsh Bridge. Court Down. Weir Cleeve.
Length: Medium. 4 miles/6¹/₂km
Difficulty: Moderate
Maps: Pathfinder SS82/92; Landranger 181

START. Dulverton car park. Map Ref. 913279. It is said that in Dulverton "the Lion lies down with the Lamb". This as you might expect refers to two pubs that could be found there! Sadly, The Lamb is no longer an inn but has been converted into flats; such are the ways of the world!

Set off by crossing over the bridge and turning right up the lane past some cottages. Now instead of turning up the pack-horse track to the left used in Walk 27, take the lower right-hand fork after the thatched cottage. You can look across at Dulverton from here.

Burridge Wood was given to the public by two generous benefactors Miss B.K.Abbot and Mr A.Herbert and there is a plaque on the left of the path that commemorates this gift.

The Barle seems to be like a necklace with Iron Age hill forts the pearls strung on it. Oldberry Castle is another of these and you will remember Brewer's Castle and Mounsey Castle just upstream and, of course, Cow Castle. It is possible to climb on up through the woods to have a look at Oldberry Castle where the earth banks are still visible. This is an area where rhododendrons thrive and once they take hold they become a menace, spreading and choking other vegetation, almost like the triffids! Red deer

The Barle at Dulverton

can sometimes be seen in Burridge Wood.

The path runs by meadows and then comes quite close to the river bank for a while, with a few ups and downs. Over a stream and past a conifer plantation until you come to Kennel Farm. This was part of the Northmoor Estate once owned by Sir Frederick Wills, one of the Bristol tobacco family. The pack of foxhounds from the estate were kennelled here.

Go through the farmyard to the road and turn right down to the bridge which you cross. However, just before you do cross keep an eye out for some ruins on your right; they are all that are left of a small chapel built by a Mr Locke in the nineteenth century.

There are, in fact, two bridges here. One for the road over the Barle, Marsh Bridge, is made of iron while nearby over a tributary is another ancient pack-horse bridge.

Turn right on the road, the B3223, and then take the track to the left which has a sign for Court Down.

You are now walking along through Looseall Wood. A marvellous name which suggests that pigs fed in these woods on acorns and beech mast for the word comes, as you might have guessed, from

131

the Anglo-Saxon "hlose" which means a pigsty!

It is a long pull up this stony track through delightful woods until you reach a broad track. You can, if you wish, cut half a mile off this walk by returning down this track to Dulverton. But I hope you will climb on to Court Down by turning right uphill, beyond the gate, to cross open fields. At the hedge you go right and through a gate to the concrete trig point at 1,036 feet (315m).

The views from here are tremendous to the south and west. You can see Dartmoor on fine days; a rolling, blue line of moors on the horizon, rising from the Devon countryside.

From the summit turn south and downhill and aim for a gap in the bank and if you keep the hedge on your right you should come to the track that leads to Northcombe House. The house is now a ruin, having been destroyed by fire in the mid-1980s.

After a short distance there is a chance to turn right to follow the hedge down to the track that you could have taken earlier to shorten the walk and this will lead you on down to Dulverton by turning left along it.

Below you to your right is the valley of the Barle with the steep slopes of Wier Cleeve running to the water's edge. It is a downhill run all the way now and then finally with a few ups and downs you will see Dulverton ahead.

At the school turn left and walk down past the churchyard where there once stood a 300-year-old sycamore which sadly had to be cut down in 1973. Down the steps past All Saints Church and suddenly you are in the bustling, busy, little town with the Lion Hotel and the Lamb Hotel that was, and the interesting town hall with its double flight of stairs. One more pub, the Bridge Inn, to avoid or not as the case may be, and you turn right to the car park near Exmoor House.

---

29. **Dulverton. Marsh Bridge. Castle Bridge. Tarr Steps. Withypool. Landacre Bridge. Cow Castle. Simonsbath.**
Distance: Long. 15½ miles/25km
Difficulty: Easy
Maps: Pathfinder SS82/92, SS83/93, SS63/73; Landranger 181,180

View down the Barle to Birch Cleave from Simonsbath

START. Dulverton car park. Map Ref. 913279. This is a really splendid and delightful walk that follows the beautiful valley of the Barle and offers quite a challenge, though it can be cut short at three different points. By studying the maps you will see at once that it is a route where you will have to be picked up at the end, or where you might stay a night en route and walk back the next day. As I said earlier, views walking on a return journey look very different when facing the other way.

I shall not give you details of the paths, tracks and the points of interest as they have all been dealt with in the following Walks: 28, 23, 26, 22, 20; I must ask you to turn back to each relevant section and use the correct part of the description there. The only stretch not described is the path along the Barle from Marsh Bridge to Castle Bridge. But as this is a broad forestry track there should be no problem in following it, especially with the signs and waymarks all the way, through Syds Wood, Invention Wood (why invention I wonder?), Shircombe Slade, and past Hinam Farm.

Here are the intermediate distances and grades:

To Tarr Steps. Medium. 5^3/$_4$ miles/9km. Easy.

To Withypool. Long. 9^1/$_2$ miles/15km. Easy.

To Simonsbath. Long. 15^1/$_2$ miles/25km. Easy but long of course.

Finally, you could start at Simonsbath or Withypool or Tarr Steps and follow the river down. Whichever you do, good luck!

PART FOUR:

The Brendons

THIS IS A high area to the east of the main mass of Exmoor that sadly no longer contains much real open moorland. A good deal of it has been reclaimed and fenced in, or has been planted with conifer forests. However, with its history of mining there are a few walks that are most interesting and worthwhile.

---

30. **Raleigh's Cross Inn. Beulah Chapel. The Incline. Western Cliff Wood. Broadfield Wood. Comberow Farm. Pitt Mill Farm. Sticklepath.**
Distance: Medium. 6½ miles/10½km
Difficulty: Moderate
Maps: Pathfinder ST03/13; Landranger 181

START. Raleigh's Cross Inn. Map Ref. 039345. This is an historic place but the modern-looking inn with its car parks, children's play area and beer garden does not reflect this. It certainly is a gateway to both the Brendons and Exmoor and stands just on the boundary of the national park. It was a stopping place for drovers and pack-horse men on their way to and from Bampton and other market towns. The August Sheep Fair is still held nearby each year in late summer and autumn and the farmers of Exmoor and other areas come here to this traditional sheep sale held in a large field. The plinth of the original stone cross stands in front of the hotel. Why 'Raleigh's' Cross, is not certain, but tradition has it that the body of Simon de Raleigh, who was killed on the campaign in France in 1387, rested here on its journey back to his home, in the Manor of Nettlecombe.

Also to be seen here is a pillbox from the Second World War which still brings back a strange flood of memories for many people.

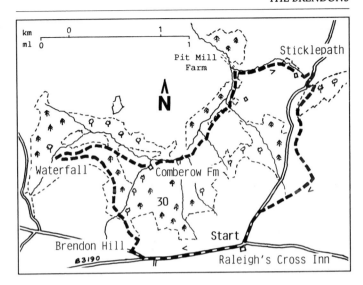

Standing behind it is a modern fire basket on a beacon put up in 1988 to commemorate the 400th anniversary of the defeat of the Spanish Armada. There were beacons near here on Elworthy Barrows from the early days and they were used right up until Napoleonic times.

Wheddon Cross is the nearest village with pubs, cafes, shops and a post office. How this name came about is not certain. It could mean 'wheat grown on a hill', but more likely 'wet hill' from the Anglo-Saxon 'Wed-don'. The importance of this crossing place of roads is obvious.

There is nothing for it but to set off along the road to the west. At least it is flat, but as it is a busy, straight road do keep well in to the side, as cars fly along here at high speed. You will pass a sign on your right that points the way to Roadwater via Comberow, so you could take that path if you wished. There are red waymarks to guide you. But I hope you will go on, for after about a kilometre from Raleigh's Cross you will come to a fork in the road and lying in the fork is the small Methodist Beulah Chapel built in 1861 for the Welsh and Cornish miners who worked here. You will find details of this industry in the introduction (see p30).

Engine House of the iron ore mine at Burrow Farm

Walk down the right-hand fork (the Wheddon Cross Road) and about 150 yards on your right there is a right of way that cuts down by a hedge to the plantation below Sea View House. The gate into the field from the road has a No Parking sign on it and just inside on the left, a bridle-path sign. Follow the hedge round to the left into the corner by the larches and beeches and you will find a gate leading onto a broad grassy track by the larch plantation. Follow this north-west until you get to a corrugated iron shed. Push through the nettles to the gate beyond and onto a steep track that drops down until you link up with the earlier track mentioned, with red waymarks, when you reach the incline of the old mineral railway. (Please turn back to the introduction to read about this incredible engineering feat.) If you are feeling strong you could walk back up the incline to have a look at the engine and winding gear house at the top. Or indeed, you could have continued along the road to look at the engine house first and then walked on down the incline to join the route here.

Cross the incline. The path to follow is obvious as you go through forestry plantations and across extremely steep slopes. After a gate the actual path begins to drop steeply down. There is a left turn by a sign and then another steep section down followed by a rise. Soon you will hear and then see a fantastic 50-foot waterfall cascading down a sheer rock face on your left.

The path more or less contours round the head of two combes and you pass a ruined cottage on your left. At the fork the sign tells you that the right-hand path is the way to go for Comberow Farm, which you will see after a while to your right. Soon you cross the stream, which you will have seen back by the ruined cottage, after swinging sharp right. The incline started at this point and was linked to the ordinary railway that came as far as here from Watchet. Some of the railway buildings still stand.

Turn left after crossing the bridge and follow the sign for Roadwater. The path now follows the track of the old railway and therefore is level. Go on past a cottage by the stream until you come to Pitt Mill Farm. Here you turn right, off the old railway track and climb on a winding path through Pit Wood until you reach another path with yellow waymarks.

Follow this now through fields and gates until you arrive at a lane. Turn right onto the lane and do not follow the yellow waymarks any more but go on to meet the B3190 road. Turn right and walk along the road for some 250 yards when you will see a sign to your left that says Monksilver and Raleigh's Cross. After a cottage the path forks right, which you take and there will be red waymarks now to guide you back to the start.

It is a slow and steady climb with some fine views away to your right and you soon come to Colton Lane and by following signs to Raleigh's Cross you will be back at your car in no time.

This walk, as you will have realized when you have finished it, took you off the edge of the north-facing escarpment of the Brendons with, of course, your having to climb back up again. Most of the paths used are marked by green or red right of way dots on your maps.

The Naked Boy Stone on the Brendons (situated half a mile south of the Raleigh's Cross Inn) marking the meeting point of parishes. Legend has it that during the beating of the parish bounds a youngster was made to stand naked on the stone or walk round it! Another story is that, at midnight a drunkard turned to stone is supposed to run down to running water to quench his terrible thirst.

---

31. **Kennisham Hill Wood. Lype Hill. Pitleigh. Cutcombe. Putham Ford. Hart Cleeve. Lype Common.**
Distance: Long. 7¹/₂ miles / 12km
Difficulty: Moderate
Maps: Pathfinder SS83/93; Landranger 181

START. The car park and picnic site built by the Forestry Commission on the edge of Kennisham Hill Wood. Map Ref. 964358 opposite the road junction to Brompton Regis, Exton and Bridgetown. These villages with Wheddon Cross are the nearest to the start for the various facilities you might need.

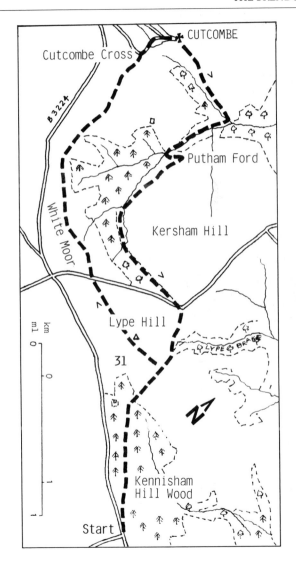

Set off along the wide forestry track to the north-west that gradually leads you away from the road. Off to your right, deep in the trees, there are the ruins of a disused mine.

Go out through the gate at the end of the forest and leave the farm and the radio mast on your left as you cross a field. Turn right after the next gate and go to the corner of the field. Follow the fence and again through another gate.

Red waymarks should show you the way to Wheddon Cross and you turn left uphill towards Lype Hill though there is no actual path to follow. You will go through another gate following the red marks. A path now leads you on to the summit with its trig point at 1,390 feet (423m).

This is the highest point of the Brendons and the views are remarkable. You can look across Devon to Dartmoor, over the levels of Somerset to the Quantocks and Mendips. To the north you will see Bossington and Selworthy and farther still the Bristol Channel and the distant mountains of Wales. North-west is Dunkery Beacon, the only other high summit at this eastern end of Exmoor. This is an area that is not often visited and when I was last here I did not see a single other person on this walk, even in high summer.

Continue over the summit of Lype Hill, a strange name that probably means at the foot of a hill. There is a small tumulus to your left. Red waymarks will take you down to the road that leads to Timberscombe, which you cross and again follow the signs for Wheddon Cross through a gate, still with red waymarks to guide you. You go first left and then back for Cutcombe Cross.

After White Moor drop gently down to Pitleigh and the track takes you to a tall gate and then moves to the higher side of the hedge. After crossing several fields and walking beside hedges you come to a lane that leads you to Cutcombe Cross and the motor road. You could turn right here and walk down Putham Lane past the old quarries to Putham Ford but you would miss something interesting.

Instead, walk down the road to Cutcombe itself. There is a feeling that this is quite a remote village because it lies on a cul-de-sac and not many people come out to it unless they live here. In Norman times this parish was included in the Forest of Exmoor.

Take the lane to the right where the road takes a hair-pin bend left and walk past the church which is pleasant enough, in a fine position looking over the valley. Perhaps the most interesting features are the two gargoyles on the tower.

Opposite the church go through the first gate and walk across to the stile in the far left-hand corner. After a while walk down to another gate and then aim at a gap in the bank of trees and follow the overgrown track down to the river.

You will soon see quite extensive ruins hidden in the undergrowth in this area. These are the remains of Stowey Mill. Obviously it was once an important mill as the large ruins show and the fact that many tracks focus here. Stowey means a 'stony track' and is a name that occurs quite a lot on Exmoor and the Quantocks.

The path goes all round the ruins but then runs off left through some trees and joins quite a large track along the true left bank of the river through Putham Woods.

At Putham Ford, Putham Lane, which you might have followed, comes in from the right, but now cross the river by the ford and follow the lane opposite uphill. There are yellow waymarks that follow the true right bank of the river in the forest and you could take that route is you wished. If not, then after 200 yards along the lane turn in right to follow the track across fields.

This track gently converges with Highley Plantation and then passes through woodland after about half a mile, where you go through a gate down to the stream.

Cross the stream and once again aim at a gap in a line of beeches, after which you turn left and follow the line of trees. You soon join a yellow waymarked path at a stile and after a while you will come to a forestry track, rather surprisingly signposted Wheddon Cross as you are, in fact, walking in the opposite direction! As you climb up to Hart Cleeve, once again there are fine views to the Bristol Channel, Bossington and back to Dunkery.

When you reach the Timberscombe road turn left along it for a short while and then right onto a track with yellow waymarks just before a thatched house. The signs say Luxborough.

You pass the head of Lype Brake, quite a deep combe, and through a gate. You can now link up with your outward journey on Lype Common and return over the fields with the farm and radio mast to your right and follow the broad track through the forest back to the car park.

---

32. **Haddon Hill. Hartford. River Haddoe. Louisa Gate. Storridge Wood. Hartford. Wimbleball Reservoir. Upton Cleave.**
Distance: Long. 8½ miles/13¾km
Difficulty: Moderate
Maps: Pathfinder SS82/92; Landranger 181

START. The car park on the corner of the B3190 road. Map Ref. 970285. Dulverton and Bampton (though it is outside the national park) are probably the nearest towns for facilities, but there are quite a few small hamlets dotted around the area, some with pubs, and there are quite a few B&Bs near here.

As always it is possible to shorten this walk and start at various different places. For example you could start at Hartford or Bury or Louisa Gate.

Climb the stile and turn left along the grassy track towards the trig point of Haddon Hill, Hadborough 1,163 feet (345m).

This is another fine viewpoint and you can look across to see Dartmoor towards the south, while the Wellington Monument on the Blackdown Hills is visible across the Vale of Taunton. As always Dunkery Beacon dominates the horizon to the north-west. Below, of course, is the huge expanse of the Wimbleball Reservoir built in the seventies and finished in 1980. It holds some 4,250 million gallons and the lake created is about 370 acres in extent. Huge expanses of water are always attractive but when valleys are drowned controversy always follows. Part of a deer park, West Hill Wood and a dwelling called Steart, all lie now below the waters. (NB The reservoir does not appear on older Pathfinder Maps.)

From the summit turn downhill and follow the path with yellow waymarks but after a while on a corner off to the right ignore the two posts with yellow marks and go on down a small path through the heather to join a large track from the left. There are fine views down to the Haddeo valley with thick trees and green water meadows.

Eventually you will come to a level concrete area near the dam where there must have been buildings and works during the construction. From here follow the broad track east until you come to a tarmac road and on the opposite side you will see two large

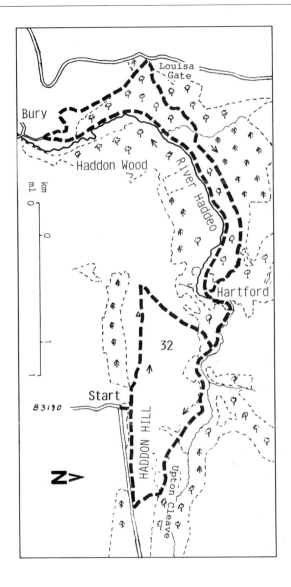

Louisa Gate

Bury

Haddon Wood

km

River Haddeo

Hartford

32

Start

B 3190

HADDON HILL

Upton Cleave

N

rocks and a sign for Upton with a track leading down to a gate. (This is the way you will go for your return much later.)

Diversion: If you want to cut this walk short you could turn right here and go uphill to follow the short route back on the road to your car. Or you could go across the road and on the track for Upton that, as I said, you will follow at the end of this walk.

To go on, turn left down the road to the dam. It is very impressive, 160 feet high (49m). It blocks the Haddeo River, of course, that continues as the overflow from the dam and tumbles down into the lovely wooded valley. You can walk onto the dam if you wish.

On now by following the road down from the dam and when you reach Hartford cross the river by the bridge; there is a ford here, too, downstream. The hamlet is very small with only a few houses and is on a cul-de-sac which must give the inhabitants a splendid feeling of isolation.

The route now goes by Hartford Lodge and then follows the Haddeo along Lady Harriet's Drive. *A brief pause while I tell you about the name Haddeo and then Lady Harriet! Haddeo comes from the Anglo-Saxon or Old English 'had' a head and 'eo' water, so it means headwater or in other words the main river in the area. The carriageway all along the river from Pixton Park and then on to Upton was constructed in honour of the great bravery of Lady Harriet Acland who rescued and looked after her wounded husband, Colonel Acland, when he was captured by the French during the war in America.*

Obviously the drive is easy to follow and it is a delightful walk by the river along Hartford Bottom, under the steep slopes of Storridge Wood. You cross a couple of side streams, one coming down from Lyncombe. By Clammer there are the first houses to be seen on this isolated route after which there are green water meadows.

The valley has opened up now and after swinging right you find a gate by a lodge. Go through the gate and turn right.

It is a steep climb up along the sunken track of Hartford Drive. To the left there are views down to Bury (there is a fine Iron Age earthworks in a superb position on a spur above the Exe near here - Bury Castle Map Ref. 938269). Off to your right there are the woods of Swinescleeve. I needn't tell you what that name means! Oaks for acorns and beech mast must have made fine fodder for the herds of pigs.

Packhorse bridge and ford at Bury

At the top, the path levels out by a fir plantation and you come to Louisa Gate. This name is also to do with pigs and comes from 'Lousy Gate' which is a Somerset dialect word for pigsty and of course the gate leads on down to Swinescleeve!

From the gate you have to follow the signs for Hartford and Upton and there are yellow waymarks to guide you. It is a marvellous walk with whortleberry plants, rhododendrons and oaks to pass and a wide range of woodland birds to see and hear. There are occasional glimpses across to Haddon Hill where you started.

Soon you will drop down into Lyncombe where you cross the stream. Go up steeply now without taking any of the left or right paths and after some more rhododendrons the path becomes wider and follows the bank along Storridge Plantations.

Storridge Lane comes in from the left and after a while, near a field, you will find yourself on a sunken track that drops down steeply through the woods and on down to Hartford; waymarks and signs all the way.

At Hartford retrace your steps back to the dam and follow the road east and uphill from there. Turn left by the rocks and the sign

Wimbleball Lake

for Upton and then on through the gate which is marked Lady Harriet's Drive and you will realize that you have joined that same carriage-way you used earlier when you were going along towards Bury. You cross the field and go down to the water.

It is a grand walk along the lake, partly through woods. On the far side of the reservoir you will have seen Upton Farm and rather surprisingly a church tower standing in the middle of a field! *This is all that remains of St James's Church. This fourteenth century church having been restored in 1796 was finally closed down in 1867 when they built a new church nearer the road. However, they moved the Norman font and the three bells to the new church and left the tower standing.*

Go along the edge of the woods in Upton Cleave. These were all part of a deer park that lay in the now flooded valley which drops steeply down to your left. Turn right and climb uphill on the path with blue waymarks. This will bring you almost up to the road opposite the woods called Britannia's Shield. How it got this name becomes apparent if you look at it on the 1:25,000 maps!

Finally, turn right along the track that runs parallel to the road and this brings you back to your car at the car park.

PART FIVE:

The Coast

ONE OF THE delights of Exmoor National Park is that it runs right to the edge of the Bristol Channel with huge plunging cliffs and whale-back hills. Of course, there is the Coastal Path and there is an excellent book that gives you the details of the walk along it: Martin Collins, *South West Way* Vol 1 (Cicerone Press). I shall link up with some of this coastal path in my efforts to work out circular routes but if you have the time you might well enjoy walking the whole of the Exmoor section of this Path from Minehead to Combe Martin. You would probably have to break it up into sections and stay for nights on the way at B&Bs or hotels as it is 34 miles or almost 55kms with a great number of ups and downs and zig-zags! (Landslip near Culbone may actually have increased this distance.)

---

33. **Holdstone Down**
Distance: Short. 2¹/₄ miles/3¹/₂km
Difficulty: Easy
Maps: Pathfinder SS64/74; Landranger 180

START. The car park in a quarry off the Trentishoe Road. Map Ref. 623474. Combe Martin is the nearest town for all the facilities you might need, though there is café up the road towards Trentishoe that you will pass on the walk. The little hamlet of Trentishoe was part of the parish of a courageous, likeable priest who later became a bishop, Bishop Hannington. He was killed in his African diocese but when he worked on Exmoor he spent a lot of time walking in his parishes getting to know not only his people, but the cliffs and moors as well. He must have looked quite a sight as he strode around dressed in "a pair of Bedford cord knee-breeches, yellow in colour, continued below with yellow Sussex gaiters with brass

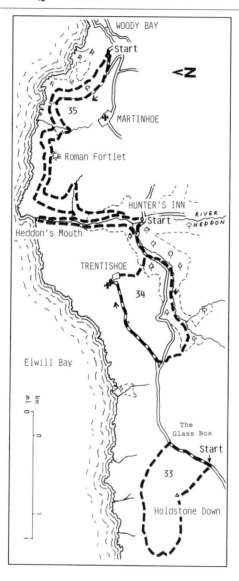

buttons." On his top he wore a black jerkin and an ecclesiastical waistcoat! Quite clearly a man who was loved and admired by his parishioners.

I have started these coastal walks with a short, easy one, with magnificent views, right on the extreme west end of the national park. There is not much to tell you about the area other than to point out the huge views, which you can hardly miss and to detail the route which is on National Trust land. It would be a good post-prandial stroll!

Set off from the car park on the path with the sign and walk up to another smaller quarry. After a while a smaller path goes on up to the summit of Holdstone Down where you will find great heaps of stones, Bronze Age cairns which also occur on Great Hangman and Trentishoe Down, to your left and right. What about the name Holdstone? More Anglo-Saxon - 'heald' and 'stan' meaning sloping ground with stones! It is a bare, open summit and is considered to be a holy summit by an obscure group known as the Aetherius Society who meet here on occasions.

This is the finest viewpoint of all but if you can drag yourself away follow the stony path off to the left down the hill. When you come to the dilapidated stone wall turn left and get through a gap to continue downhill and you will see one of the Coastal Path signs. Turn right here.

As the large track begins to climb uphill around the edge of Holdstone Down you can look down into the extremely steep gorge of Sherrycombe, indeed the steepest combe in the Exmoor National Park and the name obviously means just that.

Keep climbing gently, enjoying the breath-taking panorama across the Bristol Channel. There is a sheer drop on your left running down to the rocks below, two of which are called the Mare and Colt.

Soon you climb back to the road past the bungalow that serves refreshments and another aptly called the Glass Box. Turn right and a short walk along the road will get you back to your car.

---

34. **Hunter's Inn. Trentishoe Down. Trentishoe. Heddon's Mouth.**
Distance: Medium. $4^{1}/_2$ miles/$7^{1}/_4$km
Difficulty: Easy
Maps: Pathfinder SS64/74; Landranger 180

START. The car park opposite the Hunter's Inn. Map Ref. 655482. There are refreshments, toilets and shops to be found at the start and, of course, the inn and hotel itself, otherwise Lynton is about six miles away.

This is another well-known walking area and many routes have been described radiating from here, so there is a chance to work out several variations for yourself.

From the car park set off left past The Hunter's Inn and go over the two bridges and then turn left down a lane which is signposted to Trentishoe Mill. You must then bear left again off the lane and follow a path that runs almost parallel to it with the stream rippling down beside you just to the left. The path runs through woodland mainly made up of oaks. You will pass what looks like a standing stone but in fact was an old gatepost and an ancient boundary bank running up to your right.

At the junction, go left and then immediately right over a stile to climb steeply up through more oaks to emerge through bracken onto the open hillside that will lead you up to Trentishoe Down. Follow round the hill to the right and you reach the road. There are good views from here looking back inland to the western end of high Exmoor. Cross straight over the main road that comes up from The Hunter's Inn and walk down the small lane ahead that cuts off the corner. You soon come to Trentishoe Lane which you have to follow, I'm afraid, for about $^3/_4$ mile down to the tiny hamlet of Trentishoe itself; luckily there should not be too many cars.

The village was mentioned in the Domesday Book and was called Trendesholt and means spur on the round hill or even fort on the hill. It comes from the Anglo-Saxon 'trendel', a circle.

I mentioned Bishop Hannington in the introduction to Walk 33 and now you will pass the delightful, little church on the left where he was the priest in his early years. It is one of the smallest in Devon and worth popping in to have a look round. One of the splendid features is a little minstrels' gallery built in 1731. The balcony has a hole cut in it so that the bow of the double bass or cello player could move backwards and forwards without hitting it; what a marvellous idea! Like so many villages near the sea in Devon and Cornwall there are smugglers' tales and it is said that they used the tower of this church to hide their contraband!

Walk past the church and the few houses and swing round south down the lane. Just before the bridge turn in left through the gate with the sign that says 'Footpath to Heddon's Mouth'.

Follow the track down and round and you will soon see the enormously impressive gorge of Heddon's Mouth Cleave, nearly 700 feet deep. *The name may come from the Celtic 'etin' a giant, but heddon can also mean a heath hill, though the west side is so steep not much grows at all there. Being so deep the valley is very sheltered and warm and on the east side gorse and heather cover the slope in such a blaze of vivid yellow and purple in late summer, that if you made a painting of it people would say that you were exaggerating and making it too chocolate boxy! Grey scree slopes run down over the path in some places. Keep an eye out for dippers and grey wagtails.*

Walk past the footbridge over which you could be returning and go on down to the mouth itself, where the River Heddon, that rises almost up on Challacombe beyond Parracombe, reaches the sea. *When you look back up the cleave it makes one realize the enormous power of water to have gouged out this valley over the thousands of years. If a storm is blowing this is an impressive place to be, with huge waves thundering in onto the beach. High above you to the north-east is Highveer Point, a bleak, rugged fortress of rock, the most stark and fearful headland on this coast for many miles.*

There are the remains of a lime kiln here and coasters used to arrive and anchor off-shore from south Wales with loads of limestone and coal to be unloaded and burnt in the kiln. The resulting ash was used on the fields; you'll remember that Frederic Knight set about improving his land with lime to cut down the acidity. The little ships returned to Wales with pit props from the Exmoor forests, the produce from coppicing. It was cheaper to bring the limestone and coal to be burnt in the kilns here rather than transporting it by land on the bad roads that existed at that time.

If the River Heddon is not in flood you could cross carefully by the stepping stones for the return journey upstream. If you cannot get over or do not wish to, then turn back and walk to the footbridge which you cross to follow the path along the true right bank of the river. Just after you pass Hill Brook running down from your left, you will see the coastal path climbing up to Highveer Point. It follows the old carriage road to Woody Bay past the Roman fort known as the Beacon - one of only two bits of evidence of the Romans on Exmoor. What a trip it must have been by coach or carriage along the steep track! You climb on now, slightly uphill and through a gate. Finally turn right and left to the road and then to the car park near The Hunter's Inn. Any strange cries you may hear are not stranded tourists but the peacocks they keep nearby!

---

35. **Woody Bay. The Beacon. The Hunter's Inn. Great Burland Rocks.**
Distance: Medium. 5 miles/8km
Difficulty: Easy
Maps: Pathfinder SS64/74; Landranger 180

START. Woody Bay National Trust car park. Map Ref. 676486. You can get refreshments at The Hunter's Inn at the half way mark but otherwise Lynton is the nearest town with all the facilities you might need. A solicitor, in the early days of this century, tried to turn Woody Bay into another Lynmouth, with an eye to the tourist trade. He built a pier and paddle steamers called here with loads of trippers for teas; luckily the whole project failed and Woody Bay remains unspoilt. This is a walk that returns along the same cliffs but by a different path.

Set off west along the road from the car park to the hairpin bend where you will see a gate with the sign for the coast path. This is a broad easy track that contours round the steep ground and cliffs. There are tremendous views from this point on and you can look down on the path that you will use for the return journey. After a while you cross Hollow Brook, another deep cleft that runs down to the sea. The brook rises near Martinhoe above. The track runs past the Roman fort. The Beacon was used as a look-out post and signal station where they could keep an eye on the unconquered tribes of south Wales.

After another contour round Hill Brook the track starts a slow and steady descent to the south into the steep-sided Heddon valley and finally through trees to reach The Hunter's Inn. There is a chance to get refreshments here before you start back down Heddon Cleave.

The choice is yours, if you do not stop at the inn then you can turn right to follow the path along the true right (east) bank of the River Heddon. If you have been to the inn then go back up the road and turn left.

After just over half a mile you will come to the right fork that was the old carriageway to Woody Bay which you take. This is a long, slanting, climbing path that runs towards Highveer Point and Rocks, a wild and savage place. You are now on the path that you saw from the higher track on the outward journey. You pass Great Burland Rocks and The Cow and Calf below.

Soon you come to the waterfall in Hollow Brook Combe and the path runs quite close to the edge of the cliffs. This is a lovely corner with woods.

With Wringapeak to your left, you enter West Woodybay Wood, which was badly devastated in the storms and blizzards of December 1981, and pass quite close to Martinhoe Manor before you eventually reach the road at another hairpin bend. Turn right and you will soon be up the hill and back to your car.

---

36.   **Lynmouth. Watersmeet. Rockford. Hillsford. Myrtleberry Cleave. Lynbridge. Lynton.**
Distance: Long. 7½ miles/12km
Difficulty: Easy/Moderate
Maps: Pathfinder SS64/74; Landranger 180

START. At Lyndale Cross car park near the bridge over the East Lyn River. Map Ref. 724496. Shops, cafes etc at Lynton and Lynmouth, cafe at Watersmeet, pub with excellent meals at Rockford.

Cross the bridge and follow a road, then a path, along the true

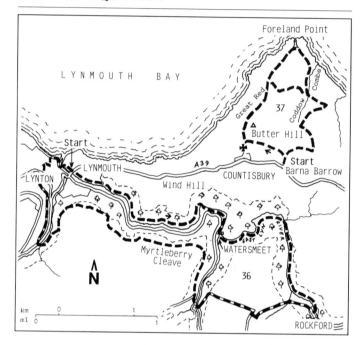

right bank of the river past Woodside Bridge and continue to the next bridge, Black Pool Bridge, which is crossed. *The thickly wooded valley is virtually a gorge and the river a boulder-strewn torrent. It is an easy matter to imagine the devastation caused in August 1952 when, after exceptionally heavy rainfall on the moors, the East and West Lyn rivers poured an estimated ninety million tons of water down onto the little town. Thirty four people lost their lives that night as buildings crumpled like packs of cards. On the way along the river bank look out for an old mineral water bottle cemented into the rock - a momento of the mineral water bottling plant that stood on this spot until it was swept away by the great flood.*

Continue past Lynrock Bridge to a great bend in the river where there is a clearing with a small cottage and across the river a view up Chisel Combe towards Countisbury. Herons can sometimes be seen here. The path continues to turn, goes past yet another bridge and fetches up at Watersmeet, where the Hoaroak Water meets the East Lyn. Cross the bridge here for the excellent cafe and shop owned by the National Trust.

Watersmeet House was built as a fishing lodge in 1830. The huge tree dominating the lawn is a Monterey Pine, Pinus radiata. Note the replacement tree already planted - farther away from the house!

It is worth a short diversion up the Hoaroak to look at the waterfall, then return to the bridge by the house, but instead of crossing it, follow the river path upstream to a beautifully restored lime kiln complex. Continue through the woods to Ash Bridge and cross the river to follow the true right bank to Rockford where another bridge leads back across the river to the welcome inn.

There is now, unfortunately, a mile of road walking, though not without interest. First the road climbs very steeply towards St Brendan's Church; a strange place to build a church since there's hardly another habitation in sight. At the junction beyond the church turn right, then follow the road sharp left and descend to Hillsford Bridge, which crosses Hoaroak Water.

Diversion: There is plenty of car parking at Hillsford Bridge. One could be picked up here, or start from here and walk down to Lynmouth. In either case Hoaroak Water could be followed between Hillsford Bridge and Watersmeet.

Main Walk Continued: Across the bridge is the main A39 road. Follow it very steeply up for a few yards to a distinct sharp bend where there is obvious access to a path on the right. It has a National Trust sign and is also marked for the Two Moors Way. The path goes past ancient earthworks, breaks free from the woods, and gives truly sensational views across the East Lyn to Countisbury and beyond. This is Myrtleberry Cleave; a high level walk which is a complete contrast to the enclosed river walk done earlier.

The path follows the top of a very steep sided valley (the East Lyn). It goes up and down a bit, zigzags, crosses a deep gully and finally splits into two. The path to the right (signposted Lynmouth) plunges down past the rocks of Oxen Tor directly into Lynmouth, but to lengthen the walk follow the left-hand path round Summerhouse Hill to Lyn Bridge. This part is known as Lyn Cleave and from it there are remarkable views of Lynmouth, Lynton and the Foreland.

Cross the road after the bridge and follow a narrow alleyway into the town of Lynton, past the youth hostel. To find the upper terminus of the Cliff Railway go down Queen Street to Lee Road where it is down a little side street almost opposite, left.

The Cliff Railway was built in 1890 by a local builder, Bob Jones, primarily to lift building materials up the 500ft cliff to Lynton from the harbour at Lynmouth. The gradient is 1:1.75, but the road gradient is 1:5 at its best, which was hard work for horse-drawn loads. There are two carriages, each capable of holding forty passengers, fastened to an endless cable. The weight of the descending carriage pulls up the ascending one, aided by a ballast tank holding 2$\frac{1}{2}$ tons of water, which is filled at the top station. The journey takes about three minutes and the service operates every few minutes until 8pm in high season and 7pm other times. On Sunday, June to September only, there is a limited service. It is closed for maintenance from January to Easter.

Alternately, instead of the Cliff Railway it is possible to descend a steep zigzag path to the bottom station. Where Queen Street meets Lee Road turn right and then left to go downhill on the North Walk. A few yards down this cut away on a path, right, and follow zigzags down to the bottom.

From the bottom station of the railway (or path end) follow the Esplanade to the harbour and walk through the town to the car park at Lyndale Cross. Time should be allowed for this!

---

37. Barna Barrow. Butter Hill. Great Red. The Foreland. Private Road from Foreland Lighthouse.
Distance: Medium. 3 miles / 4$\frac{3}{4}$km
Difficulty: Moderate
Maps: Pathfinder SS64/74; Landranger 180

START. Car park just off the A39 near Barna Barrow. Map Ref. 753496. Lynmouth is the nearest town with all facilities, but Countisbury is just off the route and is well worth a visit.

The car park itself is a splendid vantage point with huge views south to a lot of Exmoor you might have visited. Lynton on its hill and joined to Lynmouth by the cliff railway is visible; this long

The Rhenish Tower, Lynmouth built originally in 1860
by a retired general to store sea water for indoor bathing;
rebuilt after the floods in 1952.

established holiday resort was used by the better-off well before
"package deal" holidays for the masses were ever thought of.

Set off north through the gate and turn left to walk on the short
turf so typical of cliff tops in the south-west, along the wall. You will
see that a lot of the land along the cliffs and on Exmoor itself is
owned by the National Trust; what an excellent thing it is, that large
tracts of marvellous countryside are protected and maintained for
all to use and enjoy.

You could branch off left and walk down past the little church of
St John the Evangelist to have a look round the little hamlet of
Countisbury. *Countisbury probably means "camp or fortress on the hill"*
and the name must come from the fact that there is another of these
remarkable Iron Age earthworks just west of the village on Wind Hill. It
has a unique place in history for a sudden and conclusive battle was fought
here in 878 during the reign of King Alfred. Hubba the Dane came over
from south Wales with 23 ships and landed somewhere on this coast.
Ealdorman Odda was waiting for him at what can only be Countisbury, a

fortress called, at that time, *Arx Cynui*. Hubba thought that he had an easy fight on his hands but the position of the earthworks was so difficult to attack being uphill on two sides and with ramparts over 30 feet high on the others, that he failed. Odda rushed down the slopes on the enemy and killed Hubba and all 800 of his men and captured their raven banner!

A church was probably here in Norman times but in 1796 they pulled down the old nave and built a new one, while in 1835 they took down the old tower and again put up the one you see now, deliberately low and small because of the stormy winds that crash in from the west; indeed the whole church looks pretty grey and weatherbeaten! The other building certainly worth visiting is the historic Exmoor Sandpiper, formerly the Blue Ball Inn. This is a name that you will find again on a walk in the Quantocks!

Retrace your steps out onto the open cliff top and the four-way signpost. Away to your left you will look down on Lynmouth harbour with its Rhenish Tower, built in 1860 and rebuilt after the flood of 1952. These two small towns - Lynton and Lynmouth - were almost unknown until the second half of the eighteenth and early nineteenth century when the tourists started to come here because of better roads and then railways. Even Coleridge and Southey got here, but on foot!

Walk on past Butter Hill with its trig point and the T.V. Mast. This must mean a hill with good, rich pastures for cows. The drops away to your left are spectacular, down to Sillery Sands some 800 feet below!

As the path steepens you come to a fenced-off area where a great landslide occurred called Great Red. There are seats along here for you to use if you are exhausted or giddy or just want to look at the view!

There is a choice to make now. At a signpost you can turn off right and walk across to join the lighthouse road, though there is a path that goes straight on. This path demands extreme care as it is not maintained and runs across steep and dangerous ground.

If you do not use this direct path follow the path to the right, steeply down and round the hillside to the bridge at Coddow Combe, then turn left along a private road to the north for just over a kilometre and you will arrive at the most northern tip of Devon, also owned by the National Trust. The lighthouse was built in 1900. It is a lonely, wild and savage place, best seen perhaps on days of storm when huge waves crash over the rocks and even up to the light itself from a grey and angry sea.

Whichever way you choose to reach The Foreland Lighthouse there is only one way to return and that is back along the road just described to Coddow Combe. Turn left to a finger post, then turn right to follow the road uphill. *There are exciting views towards the east and along the cliffs to Old Barrow Hill where there is another Roman fort similar to the one near Heddon Cleave. Called The Beacon, it was built for the same purpose; as a lookout and signal station of about 50 men, in case the war-like Silures came over from south Wales.*

As the road levels out with Kipscombe Farm off to your left, take a right fork across Barna Barrow which will lead you down to the car park.

---

38. **Bossington. Lynch Coombe. Church Combe. Hurlstone Point. Bossington Hill. Selworthy Beacon.**
Distance: Medium. 5 miles/8km
Difficulty: Moderate
Maps: Pathfinder SS84/94; Landranger 181

START. Bossington. National Trust car park. Map Ref. 898479. This is yet another delightful village with thatched cottages that have unusual round chimneys. Walnut trees also seem to be a feature of this area. "A dog, a wife and a walnut tree, the more you beat them the better they be"! This was once the manor of Bosa, a Saxon thane and was known as Bosinthune in the Domesday Book.

If you can prise yourself away from the tea gardens selling cream teas, then set off from the car park and go straight across onto the path that leads you to a small bridge over the stream and then through a gate. Turn right after the gate and go though a field by two walnut trees. After a while you will pass through another gate and a track from West Lynch comes in from your right and here you must turn left up the hill.

If you get a chance to stop in West Lynch this also is another pleasant hamlet with old houses. There is also a most interesting agricultural museum on the farm with rare breeds and working horses. The sixteenth

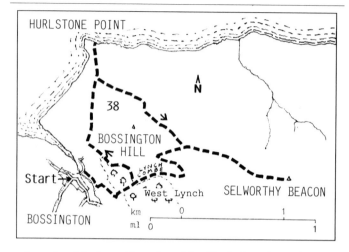

century chapel is also well worth a visit. Allerford on the road junction farther south has an excellent example of a pack-horse bridge.

But back to the walk! The signs here tell you that this is a bridle-path to Selworthy Beacon, North Hill and Minehead. It is steep and rough. Climb up and fairly soon there is another crosstracks. Turn left on the path signposted Hurlstone Point. *Lynch means a ridge found in land which has been ploughed and comes once again from the Old English or Anglo-Saxon, 'hlinc' - a ridge or bank.*

The views from this path down to the fertile plain of Porlock are good but they will be better still later on!

You soon arrive at Hurlstone Point; another rocky, wild and dangerous place both for unwary walkers and ships in storms. There is a coastguard lookout and a concrete platform where you can stand in safety to look about you.

For the return journey do not be tempted to go on and try to find your way back on the track that runs across the screes and rocks below Hurlstone Combe and then up the combe to join the next part of the route. While it is not impossible it can be a dangerous path. It is better to retrace your steps for a while and then take the steep left fork up towards Bossington Hill on the south-west edge of Hurlstone Combe (part of the coast path). This joins the dangerous path I mentioned and the two then come together to meet various other tracks large and small.

Don't take the coastal path to Minehead but cross over and take the track that runs close to the summit of Bossington Hill. A side track runs up to the actual summit and you turn right on this.

From the large cairn on the top at 850 feet (259m) the views are magnificent. Because Bossington Hill rises straight up from the Vale of Porlock which is virtually at sea level, it appears much higher than it is, both from below and when standing on it. Only Selworthy Beacon is higher around here so the views to the south-east are blocked slightly. As always, Dunkery Beacon dominates the vista when you look inland and you should make out Joaney How and Robin How and, of course, Porlock Bay and the Vale of Porlock lie 800 feet below. The steep, wooded combes of Horner, where you may have walked, are almost due south, west is Culbone and then on down the coast to The Foreland and looking the other way, out to sea, the mountains and the coastline of Wales are seen.

Porlock ('the enclosed port') is another fascinating place with old, thatched cottages and the Ship Inn where Southey stayed on his way to Lynton and Lynmouth. St Dubricius's Church ("who?" I hear you ask, and well you might!) has a strange spire on top of a low tower that was supposed to have blown down in the gales of 1700. The famous Porlock Hill used to be the Waterloo of many a motor car in the early days but it was ascended by a car for the first time in 1900. All worth a visit; but again, if you can get there out of the holiday season the crowds will have dwindled a little. Porlock Weir lies on the edge of the most marvellous wooded valleys and coastline and although I have not written about any walks there you can find your own way, I am sure, to Culbone Church, said to be the smallest in England. Charcoal burners lived and worked in the woods there and the remains of their huts and interconnecting paths are still to be seen. There are strange tales that they were lepers who never came out of the forests and a suggestion that there was a Leper's Window in Culbone Church so that they could worship there.

Come back down from the summit of Bossington Hill and get to the main track where you turn right. On for a while and at the place where one track turns very sharp right and on downhill following yellow marks, you can walk along the ridge east to Selworthy Beacon if you wish. There is another large cairn here and a trig point. This also was a signal station and beyond there are quite a number of other cairns *and Bronze Age tumuli. The only snag is that a road from Minehead runs out almost to the summit (1,011ft, 308m) and it crawls with people in the holiday period! Below is the village of Selworthy and its famous white church that will have caught your eye from many of the high points on previous walks to the south.*

Retrace your steps to the turning off left with the yellow marks running downhill to a yellow post, which you follow. Turn right by a seat until you come to a crossing of tracks with a sign that shows the way to Hurlstone Point ahead. You will recognise where you are now. Turn down left until you meet the track from West Lynch again, go through the gate and find your way back to Bossington the way you set out.

Diversion: From Selworthy Beacon follow the coastal path towards Hurlstone Point but at the head of Hurlstone Combe follow a clear path left, contouring round the hill. It crosses the deep, ferny Church Combe with excellent views and easy walking. It returns to the head of Lynch Combe, which descends to a path leading off right to Bossington. (This was the way you set out.) (Add 1½ miles/2¼km.)

PART SIX:

Exmoor Long Walks

OBVIOUSLY THERE are countless other walks on Exmoor and the Brendons that I have not included in this book but I must leave you to study your maps and maybe with the help of this guide link together some of the ones I have described and indeed, find and work out others for yourself. However, to end this section, let me give you the brief details and route plan for two historic walks that you might like to plan for yourself and follow.

---

39. Two Moors Way

On quite a number of the earlier walks you will have seen the letters M.W. carved on wooden finger-posts and indeed you will have followed the routes they point out on several occasions. This sign signifies the Two Moors Way that runs from Ivybridge, south of Dartmoor, to Lynmouth, north of Exmoor, some 102 miles (163kms). Here is the Exmoor section of this walk, which might take you two days, staying somewhere or camping en route, for it is some 22 miles (35kms).

The route crosses into the Exmoor National Park just north of West Anstey at Map Ref. 858284 so you might like to start walking from near West Anstey Barrows Map Ref. 858289 where the Two Moors Way crosses the road.

North then to Vennford Stone (venn; a fen), an old boundary marker. Over Dane's Brook, the Devon/Somerset border, by Slade Bridge ('slaed'; Anglo-Saxon, valley). Past Slade Barn. On to Hawkridge. From Hawkridge you can drop down to Tarr Steps and follow the Barle up to Withypool as you did on a previous walk, or if the Barle is in flood there is a shorter route over Parsonage Down to Westwater Farm and the shoulder of Withypool Hill. (A lot of road walking here which is best avoided.)

Set off from Withypool on the road behind the post Ofice marked *No through road*. Follow red waymarks across fields and then west along Kitridge Lane. You cross Landacre Lane that leads to the medieval bridge and follow the signs for the track that takes you down to the River Barle across moorland. By the river you link up for a while with an earlier walk from Simonsbath to Cow Castle. Cross the Barle before Cow Castle by the footbridge opposite the conifer plantation and follow a track to Horsen Farm.

From the farm walk along the drive to the road at Blue Gate and turn left towards South Molton. Go through the first gate on your right and over a heather covered field to a stream which you follow down to the River Barle again. Cross the Barle and climb on up to Cornham Farm which you pass on the west.

At the B3358, the Simonsbath/Challacombe road, turn left and take the second gate on the right. The track is signposted to Titchcombe and on to Exe Head which you will have possibly visited earlier.

The next section is well described in the walk that goes to Hoar Oak and you walk north now to Long Chains Combe, the sheepfold and indeed the Hoar Oak Tree. Cross over Hoaroak Water to the tree itself and go through the gate to the north of it. From here follow the river for a while and then cut up north onto Cheriton Ridge. This is fairly featureless country and you must be careful not to drop too far east down to Farley Water nor must you stay down too close to Hoaroak Water. A compass is a good idea for this section.

If all goes well you should hit the lane that runs down to Cheriton. Turn right down the road through the hamlet and steeply down beside Farley Water.

Walk on north on the road for Hillsford and then on the A39. After a short while on this, the Lynton and Barnstaple road, take the green lane on the right signposted 'Footpath to Lynmouth'. After a while you will see the turning to Watersmeet off to the right and you could divert to see this lovely but popular wooded spot with its cafe.

If you don't, then walk on past Myrtleberry Hangings and on to Lyn Cleave. Below is the ravine of the East Lyn which drops some 800 feet (250m) to the river and road and there are fine views from here. Finally walk down very steeply between two cottages and into Lynmouth.

40. The Perambulation of Exmoor Forest

In the introduction and a few times in the text I have mentioned the perambulation. This was necessary in medieval times when the forest law was in force and mention of it was made as early as 1300. The Warden of the Forest, who controlled all that went on in the royal hunting forest, needed to establish the boundaries periodically and to keep a check on what was going on within it. The boundaries of the forest contain a much smaller area than the modern national park, of course; only some 20,344 acres. In some parts the boundary stones or mearestones can still be seen but they are tricky to find. In other parts, especially over open moorland, there is nothing to show where it runs.

You might like to plan a walk along some or all of the forest boundary and so I shall give you the main features, names and directions to follow but I must issue a warning that there are not always rights of way that coincide with the boundary and you may have to divert so as not to trespass. Also it may not be possible to follow the boundary exactly because of rivers, fences, walls and so on, so again diversions may be necessary. Please use your maps to plan the route.

As with the Two Moors Way you may well have to do the perambulation in several sections as it is about 28 miles (45kms) right round and some of it is hard walking on the high, difficult, open moor.

A good starting point is Alderman's Barrow, Map Ref. 837424, but obviously you can cut into the circuit at any convenient point.

Set off then down the road south-west from Alderman's Barrow. On the bend, where the road turns south, the boundary goes on straight south-west to follow Sparcombe Water, the eastern branch of Ram's Combe. It crosses the Exe and then climbs Red Stone Hill.

When you reach the B3224, the Exford/Simonsbath road, it goes west for a while and then south down the road and then the lane to Thornmead Farm and over White Hill just east of Pickedstones Farm until it reaches the River Barle. (Here you may have to cross the Barle by Landacre Bridge). The boundary then goes along the

Barle to Sherdon Hutch and follows Sherdon Water up to Sherdon Rock.

Now it climbs up Dillacombe Hill, to the west of Dillacombe itself, to Hawkridge Common, over the road and on to Black Pits Plain. After Willingford Farm, still going south, the boundary arrives at Upper Willingford Bridge. You will have noticed on the 1:25,000 maps that all this part of the route is marked as a parish boundary.

At Upper Willingford Bridge the boundary now turns west along Litton Water (the upper reaches of Dane's Brook) and follows the county boundary between Devon and Somerset for a long stretch.

On to Sandyway Cross (The Sportman's Inn is just up the road from here, you'll be glad to hear!). It's a long slog on the road now, I'm afraid: Darlick Corner, Long Holcombe Cross, Kinsford Gate Cross, Setta Barrow.

Soon you'll be at the Sloley Stone and Moles Chamber which you will remember from one of the early walks in this book and the route now follows north along the muddy track and moorland to the B3358 road near Breakneck Hole.

The Edgerley Stone is on the boundary but it is impossible to follow the route directly from the stone as there is no way through the hedge! Instead you must follow the track you may have used on the walk to and from Wood Barrow and you will soon be back on the forest boundary.

From Wood Barrow on again north to Saddle Gate and the Saddle Stone that is no longer there! Here the boundary turns east and, still following the county boundary, it cuts over a series of splendid, steep combes and high, open moorland: Ruckham Combe, Thorn Hill, Warcombe Water. There are boundary stones along here but most are quite difficult to find.

Eventually the route drops down to Gammon's Corner and over Hoaroak Water to the Hoar Oak Tree. You will be in familiar country now as the forest boundary follows John Knight's great wall to Brendon Two Gates over Farley Water.

Onwards, eastwards, following Hoccombe Water (another difficult section to follow exactly) and down to Badgworthy Water.

From here again it is quite difficult to find an exact line and you may have to divert to hit one of the more obvious points and landmarks using some of the tracks and routes you may have followed in previous walks. The actual boundary follows Long Combe for a while and then runs north-east of Tom's Hill to cut across north to Stowford Bottom over Kittuck (Kite Oak, another boundary tree no longer there).

From here it crosses Chalk Water at Kittuck Barrow and follows the wall to Black Barrow. Once again you will be in country familiar from previous walks.

Finally, from Black Barrow the forest boundary swings south across awkward walking country and down to Alderman's Barrow where you started. Again there are small mearestones that are difficult to find on this section.

This Perambulation makes a grand circuit that takes you into some new country but also covers a lot of the ground that you may already have walked, so I suggest that you might like to do this walk after following some of the others first. The northern section goes across a lot of wild, open moorland and is hard walking that needs care and good route finding; take a compass and good luck!

PART SEVEN:

The Quantocks

WHEN YOU ARE driving on the M4 near Taunton and Bridgwater, the Quantocks rise up steeply to the north in a long line giving a splendid impression of height and grandeur that always makes me want to divert to explore and walk on the open moorland there. And whenever I do, I am always delighted by the area just because it does give one a feeling of a detached mountain range far higher than it really is. As with Exmoor there are steep, deep, wooded combes, mainly on the east, beech woods and hedges planted as wind-breaks, rolling open heather moorland and almost everywhere a feeling of height with tremendous views. All along the western edge there are fine country houses and in the remote little villages and hamlets, nestling below the slopes, beautiful churches, many built of the local red sandstone.

As with Exmoor the Quantocks have an extraordinary variety of scenery and landscape within their small area (38 square miles). They lie outside the Exmoor National Park but in 1957 became the first Area of Outstanding Natural Beauty in Britain and have a warden who can be contacted for information on Kingston St Mary 526.

The rocks of the Quantocks were laid down in the Devonian Period, between 350 and 400 million years ago. The Caledonian mountains of Wales, the Lake District and Scotland were to the north and to the south; across Somerset, Devon and on to France, was a shallow sea. The rocks of the Quantocks were deposited in this no man's land between the two areas. As with Exmoor, there were huge earth movements; one during the Carboniferous period, the Hercynian, that was mainly responsible for uplifting the Quantocks and the other in the Tertiary period, the Alpine.

As with many sedimentary areas there are a variety of rocks: red sandstones, limestone, Hangman grits, slates, shales, with a few small intrusions of igneous, consolidated, volcanic ash known as tuff. Again, as with Exmoor, there was no glaciation during the Ice Ages but there would have been permafrost for much of the year even when the top soil was not frozen solid.

Weathering by frost action and erosion by water carved the Quantocks into the landscape we see today with deep combes and steep slopes and open moor with an acid soil.

As I explained earlier, when dealing with Exmoor, the rocks and soils affect the vegetation which in turn affects the wildlife and all other aspects of nature. You will find heather, gorse, bracken, whortleberry, heath, and in the wetter areas sphagnum moss, bog pimpernel and so on. These, obviously, are only a few of the plants and flowers to be seen and I find that a small book on wild flowers is an important part of one's equipment when walking both on Exmoor and the Quantocks.

Thorn trees, mountain ash and hollies are found on the higher ground with the planted beeches, while in the wooded combes the oak is the natural tree and, of course man has planted large areas with conifers. Finally the rhododendron has taken over in some areas such as Vinny Combe near West Quantoxhead, creeping farther and farther up the hill, suffocating and stifling everything else as it goes. It was planted originally as cover for young breeding pheasants, I gather.

Off the high, open moorland you will be down in the deep, green, narrow lanes that run round the edges and here you will find a completely new set of flowers and plants in the warmer, lusher setting.

Buzzards, ravens, hawks, kestrels, larks, stonechats and whinchats are all to be seen and heard on the higher moor while in the wooded combes and by the streams you will come across redstarts, warblers, wagtails, flycatchers, nuthatches and woodpeckers. Again these are only a few. Quite clearly the Quantocks are a naturalist's paradise and I should add a bird book to your equipment!

Red deer are to be found, having been introduced in the last century. As you would expect, foxes and badgers also live here, along with many other mammals such as rabbits, squirrels, stoats, mice and so on.

The story of early man on the Quantocks is similar to Exmoor though not so extensive. There are Bronze Age tumuli to be seen and the circle at Trendle Ring. Iron Age forts and earthworks can be found at Dowsborough, Cockercombe and Ruborough.

Legends of Arthur and Alfred drift in and out of the stories about the Romans, the Saxons and the Danes.

Judge Jeffrey's courts in the West Country must have sent shudders and trembles through the people of the Quantocks and of course the Battle of Sedgemoor was only just down the road!

In the more peaceful times of the eighteenth and nineteenth century the Quantocks had quite a literary history with Coleridge living at Nether Stowey as did Tom Poole, while Wordsworth and his sister Dorothy rented Alfoxton House. Southey came to visit them. Other important names from that period had associations with the Quantocks - Wedgewood, Sir Humphrey Davy, Andrew Crosse.

Nowadays, as indeed from early times, farming plays an important part in the lives of Quantock people and so does forestry, while there is still an important quarry at Triscombe.

All the Quantocks are privately owned by the landowners from the big estates that lie around the edge and many farms have grazing rights for their animals on the common land. So we all walk on rights of way and permissive paths that have been agreed by the landowners and once again we should respect that.

One of the most fearful modern developments has been the four-wheeled drive vehicles that career over the maze of tracks across the Quantocks, especially when the stag hounds are out. Some even take to the open moor, creating havoc with wheel damage and erosion. There are maps which show which tracks may be used by the hunt followers but sadly many disregard them and there are always those who are not hunt followers at all and just drive their jeeps over the moor for sheer devilment.

For such a small area there is a vast amount in the Quantocks to see and find, with great variety. I hope the few walks I shall describe will whet your appetite for more: there is every chance to work out circuits of your own, as the whole of the Quantocks is criss-crossed by tracks and paths.

41. Quantock Ridge. Lydeard Hill. Will's Neck. Triscombe Stone. Crowcombe Combe Gate. Bicknoller Post. Beacon Hill. (Staple Plantation.)
Distance: Medium or Long. 6¹/₂ miles/10¹/₂km or 12 miles/19¹/₄km
Difficulty: Easy/Moderate
Maps: Pathfinder ST03/13, ST04/14; Landranger 181

START. The car park, Lydeard Hill. Map Ref. 181338. You will probably pass through West Bagborough to get to the car park and this is the nearest village with a pub and post office. I shall be writing about this hamlet in another walk. Otherwise Bishop's Lydeard is the nearest small town. The church here, made of warm, mellow red sandstone, is fine with a large tower of Gothic style. The sixteenth century carved bench-ends are worth looking at, as is the Jacobean pulpit. The West Somerset Railway starts here and runs north along the Quantocks using steam engines with their distinctive sound and smell!

Crowcombe's 14th century church built of red sandstone

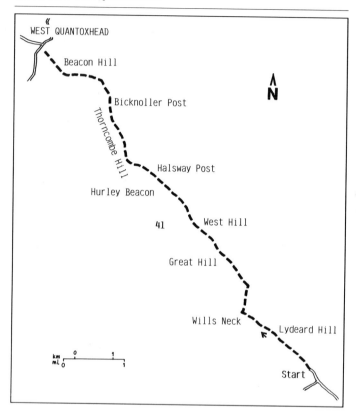

This walk is linear and unless you would prefer to retrace your steps back to the start you will require picking up at the far end. You are probably tired of reading that the views always look different on the return journey but of all the walks that I have written about, it is absolutely true for this one! The distances I have given are for either ending at the car park at Staple Plantation or turning round on Beacon Hill and walking back to the start.

The views from the car park below Lydeard Hill (1,100 feet, 335m) are tremendous, but are better to the north up on the hill itself

Trekking on the Quantocks

at 1,197 feet, 364m. It is the second highest point of the Quantocks. Northwards you can see Wales across the Bristol Channel and eastwards the Mendips are the low, blue line across on the other side of the Somerset Levels. As you climbed up to the hill you will have seen back over your shoulder the fertile patchwork quilt of the Vale of Taunton and beyond the Blackdown Hills with the Wellington Monument standing on them. On really clear days it is possible to see Dartmoor, more than 40 miles away. Closer and just north-west are the Brendons and Exmoor.

Route finding for this walk is really no problem as a broad track takes you all the way. From the gate at the car park go to the top of Lydeard Hill then descend north-west to the gate and stile at the corner of the wood on your left. The track now follows the edge of the wood with good views to Bridgwater Bay and you could hardly have failed to notice the white buildings of the Hinkley Point nuclear power station on the shore, built in 1957. The huge reactor buildings spoil this view, I'm afraid.

The left fork after the wood will take you up to Will's Neck (1,260 feet, 384m), the highest summit of the Quantocks. The views from here are even better than on Lydeard Hill, for with the extra height

Crowcombe Court

and nothing to block the line of sight you can scan the full 360 degrees; you can even add Pilsden Pen, the highest point in Dorset, to the tally. Will's Neck was once a beacon.

From Will's Neck the broad stony track takes you down north to the avenue of beeches and Triscombe Stone with its stories of the Devil and the hounds of death! It should be avoided at night! You can either continue north-west from the stone within the avenue of beeches (which could be 200 years old) or, for better views across to the Brendons and Exmoor, then it is more interesting to walk out to the left of the line of trees.

The road that you cross after a mile is the one that comes up from the village of Crowcombe, with the lovely house Crowcombe Court standing behind its gates. It is the only road across the Quantocks and goes on down to Nether Stowey. You could if you wished, therefore, cut into this walk from here, as there are plenty of parking places, and walk either north-west to Beacon Hill or south-east to Lydeard Hill.

After a while you will pass the gate and lodge of Crowcombe Park on your left and then the slight rise, again to your left, is Hurley

Beacon where there is a tumulus.

After some two miles, having passed Halsway Soggs (what a splendid name) and the steep Bicknoller Combe, you reach Bicknoller Post, one of the well-known Quantock landmarks and a meeting point of many tracks. It is said that this is where they changed the horses when the coaches came this way.

To the left of the post another steep combe drops away north-west - Weacombe Combe.

You will have crossed many tracks during this walk but the one you cross now is the Great Road that runs from Holford to West Quantock Head. This amazing track was part of the coach road from Bridgwater and Minehead. What a climb for the horses it must have been! If you are being met at the car park at Staple Plantation then you can follow the Great Road down and round now and miss out Beacon Hill, but once again you would miss a grand viewpoint from this extreme northern end of the Quantocks.

Straight on to Beacon Hill (why it has this name is obvious) and you will find a trig point at 1,023 feet (310m) and a large pile of rocks forming a cairn. The whole of this end of the Quantocks is made of the Hangman's grits that produce an acid soil with sparse vegetation. The name, by the way, comes from the fact that both Great and Little Hangman headlands in Devon are composed of this sandstone and the geologists who made this early discovery and comparison created the name.

The coast of Wales is really very close and the Brendons and Exmoor are only just over the valley to the west so you will probably have to drag yourself away from just gazing at the view but the car park is almost due west from here so you can drop down to meet your friend or about turn and set off back to Lydeard Hill!

---

42. The Two Pubs Walk! West Bagborough. (The Rising Sun). Wills's Neck. Triscombe Stone. The Blue Ball Inn. Rock Farm.

Distance: Medium 4¹/₂ miles/7¹/₄km
Difficulty: Easy, but steep start
Maps: Pathfinder ST03/13; Landranger 181

START. West Bagborough. Map Ref. 170334. This is a pleasant little hamlet well off the beaten track. The church, which you will pass later at the end of the walk, is fifteenth century and has a lovely rood screen, font cover and stained glass added in the 1920s by the artist-designer Sir Ninian Comper. If you go into the church, look out for the medieval bench-ends and the two superbly carved figures in the porch. A pottery just up the road through the village makes interesting stoneware. There is a post office here and of course The Rising Sun; what better starting place could you ask for! Careful parking is needed so as not to block the narrow road.

With iron will, leave The Rising Sun and set off up the steep and rocky track that runs just to the left of the pub. You will climb from 170m to 340m in just over a kilometre! That is about 550 feet. Near the top, the track runs by fine woodlands of beech and pine to emerge through a gate onto the main path from Lydeard Hill.

Turn left here and walk on up the track to Will's Neck with its Fire Signal Pit and tumuli and the marvellous views and then drop down to Triscombe Stone.

Running south-west from the stone there is a steep and rocky, but wide, lane that will take you down past a huge working quarry on your left. I am afraid that dust or mud and noise will spoil this part of the walk and when you are driving away in the country to the west of the Quantocks, the huge scar of the quarry is often visible as it cuts back farther and farther into Will's Neck; I hope his head won't come off completely! Watch out too for lorries.

A decision now. At the bottom of the hill is the Blue Ball Inn, a picturesque little pub with a thatched roof and a skittle alley. They serve excellent food here so if you have timed things well you could go on down to the pub for refreshments both liquid and solid!

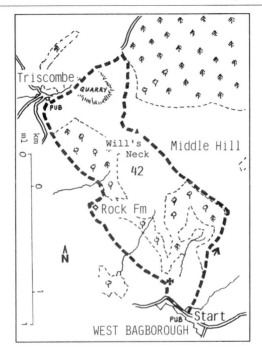

If, with great resolve, you do not wish to visit the Blue Ball Inn then just below the quarry entrance you will see a track, often very muddy, off to your left that partly contours and climbs above the pub through the woods. Take this path and you will be on the route for the return leg of the walk.

If you go to the pub then take the deep lane to the left, just beyond it, after you leave and walk for about quarter of a mile to where the lane runs close to a path in the trees to your left with steep bracken slopes climbing up to open moorland beyond. This is the path that contours round from below the quarry which you could have taken earlier. Leave the lane and join the path to walk along parallel to the lane and then, eventually, with fields to your right and steep woods to your left. There are signs for Rock Farm.

You soon reach the lane that runs down to Rock Farm. Turn right

Remains of statue overlooking the Vale of Taunton near West Bagborough

and just after the farm, on your left, there is a kissing gate. You go through it (using it as you think fit, depending on who is with you!) and follow the path to West Bagborough across and along fields.

After a while the path reaches the church mentioned earlier. As you continue along the path from the church you will notice, to your left, a really lovely, elegant Georgian house, Bagborough House, with a fine example of an Ionic colonnade on the south side.

When the path reaches the road turn back and look at the writing over the porch of the Litch Gate. It is a war memorial and also commemorates the life of Henry Robert Moore Brook-Popham of Bagborough House who was air chief marshall and lived from 1878 to 1953.

It is only a short walk now up the road to the Rising Sun and your car.

---

43. Holford Bowling Green. Dog Pound Lane. The Great Road. The Long Stone. Pardlestone Hill. Alfoxton House.
Distance: Medium. 3 miles/5km
Difficulty: Easy
Maps: Pathfinder ST04/14; Landranger 181

START. Holford Bowling Green. Map Ref. 155410. Holford itself is the nearest village with all the facilities you might need - including the Plough Inn which is said to be haunted by an eighteenth century Spanish captain who was murdered there having arrived at Watchet on a trading voyage. To reach the car park turn in by the Plough Inn and go through narrow lanes past the church and take the right fork by the thatched cottages.

Set off west along the lane to the north of the green and soon on the corner you will see the Georgian dog pound built of grey local stone that has been recently repointed. Do not follow the lane round the steep bend but branch off left on the rocky track that climbs steeply on through beech trees. This is the Great Road: it was the coach road from Bridgwater to Minehead. It is hard to imagine how the coaches were able to be pulled up this steep and stony track.

Climb on and you will be aware that away to your right is Alfoxton House standing in its deer park. It was here that William Wordsworth and his sister Dorothy lived for some time while Coleridge had a house just down the road at Nether Stowey. They spent many happy months in the Quantocks and got to know the area well. You can leave the track and reach the wire deer fence if you want to look down on the house, now a hotel, but you will be passing by it later on.

At the top of the hill you emerge out onto the open moorland with huge views out to the Bristol Channel with the two islands of Steep Holme and Flat Holm clearly visible. As always, the coast of Wales with the Black Mountains and the Brecons beyond can all be seen on fine days. This is an area of bracken, heather and gorse while a little back where the beeches ended there are rhododendrons, mountain ash and small oaks. If you meet people with mauve lips in July and August you will know that they have found ripe

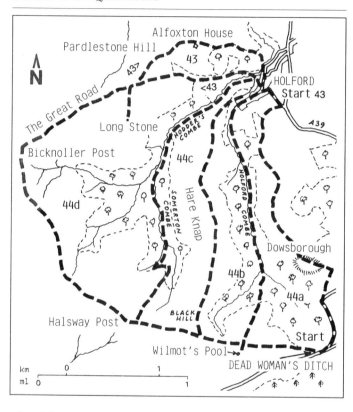

whortleberries up here!

After a further quarter mile you will see a very obvious track to your left running up the hill. Take this and walk up to the Long Stone. Nobody quite knows why it was put here at a height of 952 feet. There are a few ancient mounds just north-east of it and it is fairly close to the spring for Dens Combe or even Hodder's Combe but there is no real evidence as to its purpose. It is not very large.

Retrace your steps down to the edge of Holford Beeches. The beech-lined track that leads back to Alfoxton House is called The Avenue. You can either take that route down through the trees or stay out on the moorland and walk down Pardlestone Hill to Alfoxton House. Whichever you choose the way is obvious and soon you will join the tarmac drive that will take you round to the back of the house. It is an easy walk now along the drive through the park until you reach the gates to the hotel. Holford Glen is off to your left. Back past the dog pound and across the green to your car on the far side.

---

44. **a.** **Dead Woman's Ditch. Dowsborough. Holford. Holford Combe. Wilmot's Pool.** ($4^1/2$ miles/$17^1/4$km)

   b. **Dead Woman's Ditch. Dowsborough. Holford. Lower Hare Knap. Black Hill.** ($4^3/4$ miles/$7^3/4$km)

   c. **Dead Woman's Ditch. Dowsborough. Holford. Hodder's Combe. Somerton Combe.** ($5^1/2$ miles/9km)

   d. **Dead Woman's Ditch. Dowsborough. Holford. The Great Road. Bicknoller Post. Halsway Post.** ($6^1/2$ miles/$10^3/4$km)

All these routes are of moderate difficulty and are to be found on Pathfinder ST04/14 or Landranger 181)

START. Dead Woman's Ditch. Map Ref. 162382. There is a large car park here. From the name you might expect another gruesome story! We had a child murderer at Wheal Eliza, back on Exmoor; we have a wife murderer here! Apparently a charcoal-burner called Walford killed his wife in a terrible drunken rage as they were returning from the inn called the Castle of Comfort, now an hotel near Nether Stowey. He hid the body in the ditch which you can see to the south of the car park, but to no avail as it was soon discovered. Walford was taken and hanged at a place still called Walford's Gibbet farther down the road you will be walking along soon. The ditch is probably part of an Iron Age field system linked with Dowsborough, which you will also go through on these walks.

Nether Stowey or Crowcombe are both equidistant from the start for pubs. Nether Stowey is larger and well worth a visit. It is another

Dead Woman's Ditch

secluded, pleasant little village with a stream running down beside two of the main streets. Coleridge lived here in Lime Street, in a little house now known as Coleridge Cottage and owned by the National Trust. He was only here for three years from 1797 but he wrote some of his best works in this Quantock interlude: *The Ancient Mariner*, *Kubla Khan* and part of *Christabel*. I wonder how the country folk of Nether Stowey regarded the drug-taking Coleridge, drifting through his opium dreams, and his literary friends from Alfoxton House, the Wordsworths! Charles Lamb also came to this village. Coleridge Cottage has a room open for visitors with a lot of interesting material on display.

The church, largely rebuilt in 1851, is well out of the village on the other side of the busy A39.

The grassy mound at the southern end of the village is all that remains of Stowey Castle dating from Norman times; the ruins of the square keep are just visible. Finally, there is the information centre in the library that has leaflets about the Quantocks.

You will see that I have suggested four walks from this one starting point at Dead Woman's Ditch, each one a little longer than the other.

a) Cross the road from the car park and set off north on the old coach road to the Castle of Comfort, that drops down through oak woods. I suppose these are the woods where Walford burnt his charcoal mounds. Just after the steep corner to the right a track strikes up north getting steeper as it climbs. Keep left at the fork you come to and this leads you to Dowsborough, an Iron Age settlement at 1,093 feet; a most impressive place. A walk round the ramparts gives you some idea of the enormous efforts that must have gone into the making of such a huge earthworks. It would be hard enough with modern bulldozers and earthmovers!

Much of the fortress is covered with scrub oak but from the north-west corner, where there is a clearing, the views are tremendous over Bridgwater Bay. *There is a ghost, of course, and the settlement was once called Danesborough, after a battle in which some marauding Danes were slaughtered here. The legend goes that a young minstrel with the Danish raiding party escaped and was sheltered by a Saxon girl who, of course, fell in love with him; it was probably the love songs he played on his harp that did it. As you might expect he was betrayed and in spite of her entreaties the young minstrel was killed by the Saxons. It is his ghost that you might meet and hear as he wanders along the ramparts looking for his Saxon girl, playing on his harp and singing his love songs to her.*

One track makes a complete circuit of the ramparts, another goes in between the inner and outer earth banks and it certainly is worth spending some time here wandering around.

To continue the walk, go to the north-west corner where there is the clearing with the views and you will see the track that you need to follow dropping down over Woodlands Hill. This is more National Trust land.

The track brings you down near to the A39 road but you must turn left along the smaller road that goes on to the Bowling Green (variant c diverges here) and just after the sharp bend left you will see the lane on your left (variant b diverges here) that leads you to Combe House, now an hotel, with a waterwheel used when the building was a tannery. There are also some cottages here.

The lane soon becomes a gravel track and criss-crosses the stream as you walk on into the oak woods of steep Hodder Combe.

Eventually you come to a splendid dividing of streams and

tracks in a deep secret combe. Up to the left is Lady's Combe, to your right is Frog Combe with their gnarled and stunted oaks, hollies and rhododendrons, but you must take the central stony path which climbs up steeply in a southerly direction.

You will soon be on the high Quantock moorland with Dowsborough off to your left and fine views north once again to the Bristol Channel. Carry on over the cross tracks and wander on south to have a look at Wilmot's Pool at 1,100 feet. Sadly, with the last few years being so dry, on the occasions that I have visited this pool, usually used by ponies and deer, it has been dry.

Turn back now and return north to the cross tracks where you turn right and this will lead you to your car at Dead Woman's Ditch.

b)   Start this walk the same way as (a) so please look back for details to the place where variant b diverges.

The new route starts now. Having set off as if you were going up to Holford Combe past Combe House, about 200 yards up the lane there is a footpath to your right, nearly opposite the line of houses, that climbs steeply up to join the path that runs down to the Bowling Green car park. Turn left onto this path and be prepared for a long steady climb up to Lower Hare Knap. The track is very badly eroded here with deep ruts.

On now to Higher Knap with its tumulus. There is a grand feeling of height here with steep drops to Holford Combe on one side and Hodder's Combe and Somerton Combe on the other.

As you walk over Black Hill you reach the main east-west track and here you turn left and once again this leads you back near Wilmot's Pool (you could go and see if there is any water in it) and on to your car.

c)   Set off again as for Walks a and b. When you reach the road keep on past the turning to Holford Combe as before and you will soon come to the Holford Bowling Green car park. Stay on this side of the green and follow the track past the houses and you walk on into lovely woodland with the stream to the right of you. Keep on the main track as another forks off right over the stream to the house of Willoughby Cleeve. You will see on your right a strange eight-sided building called, for some unknown reason, The Round House, built in Georgian times.

Follow the track now into the very steep-sided Hodder's Combe with the trees of Willoughby Cleeve sweeping up the far side from the flat valley floor. You pass a ford that leads into Short Combe and then there is a dividing of the ways and valleys. Ahead is wooded Somerton Combe and this is the way you go now, but off to your half-right is Slaughterhouse Combe with a reasonable track up it and farther right, almost at right angles, Sheppard's Combe, all three deep, wooded combes where the red deer lie up during the day, as they do in many of the woods on these four walks.

You criss-cross the stream a few times as you climb up Somerton Combe and at the head the path takes a climbing zigzag and out onto open moorland to arrive at the same east-west track near Halsway Post. As before, you follow this east back to the car park.

d) This final circuit, the longest of all, covers a lot of the same ground as previous walks in the Quantocks but links them all into one so I need give you only brief directions and must ask you to look back for the information and anecdotes.

Set off from the ditch where Walford hid his murdered wife and over Dowsborough, listening hard for the gently sweet, lilting sounds of the harp! On over Woodlands Hill and down to the Holford Bowling Green. Take the road on the far side that leads to the drive of Alfoxton House, but, as for Walk 42, fork left on The Great Road by the dog pound where I am sure you will hear the ghostly scrunch of coach wheels, the crack of the whip and the faint high call of the post horn!

Climb on to Holford Beeches with a glimpse down to Alfoxton House, where you might just see William Wordsworth with Dorothy walking in the park, or indeed you might meet them by the great beeches of The Avenue.

You will pass the turning up to The Long Stone and perhaps feel the presence of Bronze Age man and ponder about why he put the stone there.

Far out on Longstone Hill the Great Road swings off right and you take the left fork to Bicknoller Post and once again hear the post horn and the chink and clink of harness as they change the horses for the final run down to Minehead.

From here swing south on the Quantock ridge track over Black

Ball Hill to Lowsey Thorn until you reach Halsway Post near Halsway Sogg, where you follow the left fork which is the track you will have joined each time to take you back to the start.

This is a fine, exciting circuit that takes in almost everything that these delightful moors, the Quantocks, can offer, except perhaps walks in the man-made coniferous forests. There are even trails there you can follow, working out circuits for yourself. You could walk to places like Rams Combe, Quantock Combe, Keeper's Combe, Two Tree Bottom and the other Iron Age settlement in Cockercombe. Like Exmoor you could keep planning walks forever and still never find and see everything there is to find and see.

A GLOSSARY OF SOME EXMOOR
AND QUANTOCK TERMS

ADIT   Horizontal tunnel made by miners into a hill or side of a gully.

ARRISH   A stubble field.

BARTON   A farmyard.

CLAPPER   A bridge made of huge slabs of stone resting on piers across rivers and streams. They are not prehistoric but were usually built on pack-horse routes across the moors and between farms.

COB   A mixture of clay and straw used in the construction of walls for houses and barns.

COMBE   A wooded, steep-sided valley usually closed at one end. The word comes from the Celtic word 'cwm'.

COMMONERS' RIGHTS
                The rights of certain farmers and landowners to graze animals on the open moor.

COURT   An enclosed yard of a farm.

DEEK   A name given to the fencing of an earth bank with stones.

DRIFT   The name given to rounding up cattle and ponies to make sure that the animals belong only to commoners who have grazing rights. Also another name for an adit in a mine.

GOYAL   A deep gully or cleft eroded by water.

HARBOURER   The hunt servant whose job it is to find out where the deer are lying up.

HOGG   A yearling sheep.

KNAP   A small, rounded hill.

TO LAY A HEDGE The art of trimming the saplings in a hedge by half cutting them and laying them horizontally so that they continue to grow.

LINHAY, LINNEY A shed with an open front usually for keeping carts, waggons or wains, but nowadays tractors.

LYNCHET   Man-made terrace.

MOOT   A tree stump after felling.

MORE	A root left underground.
PENTICE	A lean-to shed.
SELL	A circular walled enclosure usually with trees growing around it which sheep can use for shelter in blizzards.
SHIPPON	A cowshed.
SLOT	The footprint of deer.
SOIL	When a deer takes refuge in water.
TALLET	A loft in a barn or other farm building.
TEDD	To spread grass out after cutting for hay.
TUFTER	The hound that drives deer out of cover.
VUZZ	Gorse.
WHORTLEBERRY	*Vaccinium myrtillus.* Bilbery, blueberry, blaeberry. The small mauve berry that grows on Exmoor which can be gathered in July and August. Known locally as 'hurts' or 'urts'.

The author beside the Long Stone, Chapman Barrows
(see Walks 2 & 3)

USEFUL ADDRESSES AND TELEPHONE NUMBERS

Exmoor National Park Information Centres

The Exmoor National Park Authority, Exmoor House, Dulverton, Somerset.

Tel: 0398 23841. Open all year.

Visitor Centre, Dunster Steep, Dunster, Somerset. Tel: 0643 821499.

Open March - mid November.

Information Centre. County Gate. Countisbury, North Devon. Tel: 0598 7321.

Open April - end of October.

Information Centre. The Esplanade, Lynmouth, North Devon. Tel: 0598 52509.

Open April - end October.

Information Centre. Seacot, Cross Street, Combe Martin. North Devon.

Tel: 027188 3319. Open April - end September.

All postal enquiries to Exmoor House.

Guided Walks and Group Visits. Tel: 0398 23665.

Exmoor Natural History Society, 24 Staunton Road, Alcombe, Nr Minehead, Somerset.

Exmoor Society, Parish Rooms, Dulverton, Somerset.

Exmoor Tourist Association. Secretary, Mr D. Wade, Anchor Inn, Porlock Weir, Somerset.

Fisheries Officer, Wessex Water, PO Box 9, King Square, Bridgwater, Somerset.

National Trust Estate Office, Holnicote, Nr Minehead, Somerset.

Quantock Information Centre. Tel: 082345 526.

Somerset Trust for Nature Conservation, Fyne Court, Broomfield, Taunton, Somerset.

Weather Forecasts. Tel: 089814 1203.

BIBLIOGRAPHY

BLACKMORE, R.D.	Lorna Doone
BURTON, S.H.	Exmoor
DELDERFIELD, E.R.	The Lynmouth Flood Disaster
GIDDENS, C.	Flowers of Exmoor
GRINSELL, L.V.	The Archaeology of Exmoor
HODGES, C.W.	The Overland Launch
HOSKINS, W.G.	The Making of the English Landscape
JEFFRIES, Richard.	Red Deer
JONES, S.	Legends of Devon and Somerset
LAGMUIR, Eric.	Mountaincraft and Leadership
LAWRENCE, B.	Coleridge and Wordsworth in Somerset Exmoor Villages
MACDERMOT, E.T.	A History of the Forest of Exmoor
MILES, R.	The Trees and Woods of Exmoor
MORRIS, J. (Ed)	Domesday Book. Devon. Somerset
PEEL, J.H.B.	Portrait of Exmoor
MEE, A.	The King's England Series. Devon. Somerset
SELLICK, R.J.	The West Somerset Mineral Railway
WAITE, V.	Portrait of the Quantocks
WORDSWORTH, D.	Alfoxden (Alfoxdon) Journal

Many books, leaflets and pamphlets about Exmoor are published by The Exmoor Press, Dulverton, Somerset.

The volumes of *The Exmoor Review* published by The Exmoor Society, The Parish Rooms, Dulverton, Somerset, are full of interesting and important information about Exmoor.

The information centre of the E.N.P.A. at Exmoor House has a wealth of books, leaflets and pamphlets for sale.

Printed in Gt. Britain by
CARNMOR PRINT & DESIGN
95-97 LONDON RD. PRESTON